36 Views

36 Views

a play by

Naomi Iizuka

THE OVERLOOK PRESS
WOODSTOCK & NEW YORK

First published in the United States in 2003 by
The Overlook Press, Peter Mayer Publishers, Inc.
Woodstock & New York

WOODSTOCK:
One Overlook Drive
Woodstock, NY 12498
www.overlookpress.com
[for individual orders, bulk and special sales, contact our Woodstock office]

NEW YORK:
141 Wooster Street
New York, NY 10012

Library of Congress Cataloging-in-Publication Data

Iizuka, Naomi.
36 views : a play / by Naomi Iizuka. — 1st ed.
p. cm.
1. Art dealers—Drama. 2. Art historians—Drama.
3. Manuscripts, Japanese—Drama. I. Title: Thirty-six views. II. Title.
PS3559.I39A613 2003   812'.54—dc21   2003040576

Book design and type formatting by Bernard Schleifer
Manufactured in the United States of America
FIRST EDITION
1 3 5 7 9 10 8 6 4 2
ISBN 1-58567-383-8

INTRODUCTION
by Alan MacVey

In the fall of 1999 I was searching for a new play to direct the following summer at Breadloaf. I asked my colleague Naomi Iizuka if she was writing anything, and she said she had just completed a new play. A few days later she placed a copy of *36 Views* in my mailbox. I read it that night and thought it was the most beautiful new play I had encountered in many years. Over the next few months I came to view it as not just a beautiful work but as a genuinely original dramatic creation.

One of the things that makes *36 Views* unusual is that it takes its form from two very different theatrical traditions. Most audiences easily recognize the first. It is based in realism and shaped by story, character, and idea. The story of *36 Views* has several threads, but at its heart it's fairly simple. An art dealer and an art historian discover an ancient manuscript; they try to learn whether it's authentic and then deal with the results. As they make their way through the contemporary art world, they and four other characters are revealed to us a bit at a time, surprising us with their growing complexity. The play's ideas also begin to crystallize as questions: What does it mean when we say a work of art is real or fake? Do these categories mean anything beyond taste and economics? Is it possible to love another person without faking it at times? Does it matter? The playwright carefully controls her story, characters, and ideas so that every scene moves the audience forward. Each is filled with actions, reversals, events, and discoveries—all hallmarks of good drama. This makes the play accessible. On the what-happens-next level, Iizuka continually surprises without losing us. We understand her dramatic form and are at ease with it.

But *36 Views* is also part of the experimental theater tradition. Language and image are at the center of this dramatic form, which has its modern roots in Buchner and Strindberg and finds its boldest expression in the work of Gertrude Stein. In most traditional plays, language is used as a way for characters to express what they mean. In *36 Views*, as in poetry, language performs other functions as well. The sound of a word may be as important as its meaning. The feeling of a phrase—its rhythm, repetition, and development—works as music does, intuitively, aesthetically. As in Stein's plays, a sentence can be so intensely personal that it seems too distant to understand. But in its rhythms it helps accumulate energy.

The same is true of the play's many visual images. An eleventh-century Japanese woman removes layers of clothing while a contemporary male character tells an unrelated story; two nearly identical paintings, one 'real" and the other a forgery, hang facing one another; a mosaic of unrelated pieces moves together to form an almost perfect picture. These and many other images are related to the main story, but obliquely. They stand next to it, sometimes complementing, sometimes questioning events on stage. On occasion they seem to bear almost no relation to the plot at all. But they are integral to the experience the playwright is creating.

The traditional and experimental forms converge in what I consider to be the most charged scene of the play. The audience has arrived at the moment when they want to hear part of the found manuscript, which apparently is an eleventh-century "pillow book." The main character, Setzuko, is poring over its pages, and in a conventional play she would probably read a portion of it aloud to another character. But that isn't what happens. Instead, a woman dressed as an eleventh-century Japanese courtesan, played by the same actress who plays Setzuko, speaks a portion of the manuscript as if she is pouring out her heart and soul. Other actors take roles in the emerging landscape. Music, lighting, and scenic elements add to the mystery of the event, so we hardly know what we are seeing. But we do know that we are *experiencing* the manuscript, not just learning about it. It comes alive on its own terms. Yes, it reveals the psychology of the woman who discovered it, but it demands that we pay attention to it separate from her. Its language is poetic and strange. Its images are drawn from another culture. We are, unexpectedly but comfortably, in eleventh-century Japan.

Then we're back in the present. No direct reference is made to what just happened. In terms of plot the entire scene could be cut. But the event has deepened the story and its characters, and its theatrical language has revealed the soul of the play.

The scene also helps uncover another aspect of *36 Views*. The ideas at the play's center are not just discussed by the characters, as they might be in a work by Shaw. They are also embodied by its theatrical elements. In the opening scene, when a medieval woman is transformed to become a university professor, we are already forced to question our assumptions about what is real. Moments later, as characters discuss whether the art objects on stage are genuine or forgeries, we are also aware that all the props were created for the production. The pillow book is real, then a forgery, then real again, until the final scene, when we are asked to reflect on whether it, or any of what we saw, was real—which, of course, it wasn't. These scenes and many others keep the play's ideas alive in the imagination, rather than sending them to the crowded closet of the intellect.

36 Views, then, is a truly surprising work. Its complex form and the way it embodies ideas—as well as its very clever plot—keep an audience from settling back and simply watching. Viewers have to participate in its creation and are continually, pleasantly startled by what is happening on the stage and in their minds. This certainly was my experience of the play. The manuscript came to me as a gift, a gentle surprise. I read it and thought I understood it. As I worked on the play, I realized I grasped only the surface of its beauty. By the close of our summer production I again thought I understood it. But when I saw its New York premiere eighteen months later, I found that the play shimmered in my mind and seemed to resist ever being fully understood. My many experiences with *36 Views* overlapped, and, like a character in the play, I wondered if any of them was quite real.

Breadloaf, Vermont
June 2002

36 *Views* was commissioned by A.S.K. Theatre Projects in Los Angeles. The play was written under the auspices of Princeton University's Hodder Fellowship and workshopped at the McCarter Theatre, A.S.K. Theatre Project's Common Ground Festival, the Public Theatre's New Works Now, Sundance Theatre Lab, and Breadloaf.

36 *Views* was originally produced by the Public Theatre/New York Shakespeare Festival, George C. Wolfe, Producer, in association with Berkeley Repertory Company, Tony Taccone, Artistic Director, and Susan Medak, Managing Director. It premiered in New York City at the Public Theatre on March 28, 2002. It was directed by Mark Wing-Davey, with scenic design by Douglas Stein, costume design by Myung Hee Cho, lighting design by David Weiner, sound design by Matthew Spiro, and production design by Ruppert Bohle; the production stage manager was John C. McNamara. The cast was as follows:

Darius Wheeler	Stephen Lang
Setsuko Hearn	Liana Pai
John Bell	Ebon Moss-Bachrach
Claire Tsong	Elaine Tse
Elizabeth Newman-Orr	Rebecca Wisocky
Owen Matthiassen	Richard Clarke

"Only a part of what is perceived comes through the senses from the object; the remainder always comes from within."

—MATTHEW LUCKIESH, *Visual Illusions*

CHARACTERS

Darius Wheeler, a dealer of Asian arts and antiquities.

Setsuko Hearn, an assistant professor of East Asian literature.

John Bell, Darius Wheeler's assistant.

Claire Tsong, a restorer of Asian artifacts.

Elizabeth Newman-Orr, a free agent.

Owen Matthiassen, the chair of the East Asian Studies Department.

ACT ONE

Scene 1

(*Darkness. Suspended in the darkness is a hanging scroll. On the scroll is a painting of a Japanese woman in formal pose, Kamakura era, gilt background, a portrait of a lady. In the shadows is* DARIUS WHEELER. *As he speaks, he becomes more and more visible.*)

DARIUS WHEELER

True story. This is a true story.

I'm in the middle of the Doi Larng mountain range, no-man's land between Thailand and Myanmar—

Burma, end of what they call the old Elephant Trail—

Kipling country, used to be

Now—

Well, now it's something else.

I'm talking early eighties, opium in every little village east of Mae Hong Son, opium not even the half of it—sapphires, ivory, pigeon-blood rubies from the Mogok Valley—blackmarket all of it, and you could get a bullet in your brain trying to do business with these people. Some hop-head Palang with an M-16, he just blows you away on the spot, cause he thinks you're a white devil—

Or a ghost—

(*The sound of the shakuhachi flute.* SETSUKO HEARN *is revealed in Heian-era kimono, wig, and white face paint. She begins to remove her makeup and her wig.*)

DARIUS WHEELER

Cause these tribal people, they hate ghosts—

Or maybe, maybe he just doesn't like the look in your eye

Human nature

A little cultural miscommunication—

And what are you going to do about it, you're in the middle of what they call the Shan state. There are no maps for this part of the world. You disappear and that's it, you're shit out of luck, head on a pole, tiger meat—

Then again, you go in there, and you meet the right people, and maybe, say, you do some business with these people, and maybe, just maybe you come away with something so beautiful, something so incredibly beautiful, something you'd never find, not in a million years on the outside, and if you're lucky, if you're smart, you get yourself out of there in one piece. So I'm there with my Lahu guide, feeling lucky, tiny Shan village, waiting for my contact, friend of a friend . . .

(DARIUS WHEELER *continues to speak. His voice grows fainter, a distant echo.* ° *The sound of the shakuhachi flute is joined by the sound of drums.* SETSUKO HEARN *is turning. With each turn, a layer of kimono is removed. The music grows louder, the pace grows faster. The sound of wooden clappers. Silence. The sound of the shakuhachi flute, alone and unadorned.*)

DARIUS WHEELER

Unbelievable what I saw that night: Song Dynasty temple paintings, Kushan Period Buddhas almost two thousand years old. He had stuff from Angkor Wat, museum quality, objects there's no way he should've had, and I'm thinking, who are you? Who are you? Because the thing was, this was the thing, I knew, as soon I saw it, as soon as I touched it and held it in my hands, I knew it was real. No question in my mind, it was real, and if I had enough money, it was mine.

(*The sound of the shakuhachi flute ends. Hikinuki, a Kabuki costume change in which threads are pulled, and the outer kimono falls away, revealing a new costume underneath.* SETSUKO HEARN *is transformed into an urban, late twentieth-century, Western woman. The sound of wooden clappers.*)

°*The remaining section of* DARIUS WHEELER'S *monologue appears after the end of the play.*

Scene 2

(Evening. SETSUKO HEARN *and* DARIUS WHEELER *in* WHEELER's *loft space. The space is divided by translucent shoji screens. The Kamakura-era painting, the portrait of the woman in formal pose, is prominently featured. Somewhere else in the space, a party in progress. Voices, music.)*

DARIUS WHEELER

Beautiful, isn't it. Everything else I bought that night, I sold, made out like a bandit. This one I never had the heart to sell.

SETSUKO HEARN

Why is that, do you suppose?

DARIUS WHEELER

I don't know, call it an appetite for beauty.

SETSUKO HEARN

I see.

DARIUS WHEELER

Is that such a terrible thing to be? Don't we all gravitate towards beauty? Don't we all crave beautiful things? It's second nature, don't you think. I don't know that we can help ourselves.

SETSUKO HEARN

A philosopher and also quite the renegade.

DARIUS WHEELER

Oh, I don't know about that.

SETSUKO HEARN

I think you're being modest, Mr. Wheeler. I'm guessing you've had more than your share of adventures in the Orient.

DARIUS WHEELER

I have some tales to tell.

SETSUKO HEARN

I'm sure you do, all kinds of wild and woolly tales.

DARIUS WHEELER

Very wild, very woolly, yes.

SETSUKO HEARN

Let me guess: rickshaws and opium dens. A rendezvous with some shady characters on the back streets of Hong Kong, Chinese Triad types, practioners of Kung Fu. Or perhaps it was on the South China Sea, a foggy night, a sampan full of Malay pirates, inscrutable, ninja-like.

DARIUS WHEELER

Is it my imagination or are you making fun of me?

SETSUKO HEARN

Am I?

DARIUS WHEELER

You know, I think you are.

SETSUKO HEARN

I'm afraid that tales from the Orient, there's this sort of wilted quality to them.

DARIUS WHEELER

Ah.

SETSUKO HEARN

I've offended you.

DARIUS WHEELER

No, on the contrary. The ridicule, the skepticism, I find it kinda bracing. So tell me, I'm curious: am I the biggest idiot you've ever met?

SETSUKO HEARN

Let's just say, you seem to be a man with a weakness for stereotype.

DARIUS WHEELER

You know, you look very familiar to me. I can't say from where. Maybe you look like someone else.

SETSUKO HEARN

Possibly.

DARIUS WHEELER

Jakarta? Sidney?

SETSUKO HEARN

I've never been.

DARIUS WHEELER

Are you sure?

SETSUKO HEARN

Very.

DARIUS WHEELER

Maybe you have an evil twin.

SETSUKO HEARN

Maybe I am an evil twin. People make mistakes, Mr. Wheeler.
They misapprehend.

DARIUS WHEELER

I don't know why, but I feel as if I know you.

SETSUKO HEARN

You don't. Trust me. We're perfect strangers.

(*The sound of wooden clappers.*)

DARIUS WHEELER

Darius Wheeler.

SETSUKO HEARN

Setsuko Hearn.

DARIUS WHEELER

Please forgive me. I'm being a terrible host. Here I let you just
stand there without any kind of refreshment, parched, no
doubt. What are you drinking? I have this wonderful plum
wine in honor of Utagawa. Very light, very seasonal. The guy
probably prefers single malt Scotch, but what the hell. Plum
wine? Good stuff.

SETSUKO HEARN

All right.

DARIUS WHEELER

Plum wine it is.

(DARIUS WHEELER *prepares drinks, cracking ice with a pick.*)

DARIUS WHEELER

Somehow I feel like you know a lot more about me than I
know about you.

SETSUKO HEARN
Funny, I feel that way, too.

DARIUS WHEELER
So fill me in, Setsuko. Tell me something about yourself.

SETSUKO HEARN
There's nothing really to tell, I'm afraid. My life is very humdrum compared to yours. Very uneventful, very tame.

(DARIUS WHEELER's *hand slips. A cut.*)

SETSUKO HEARN
Are you all right?

DARIUS WHEELER
A little cut. It's nothing.

SETSUKO HEARN
Are you sure?

DARIUS WHEELER
Yeah, no, it's fine.

SETSUKO HEARN
You know, I actually found your story very entertaining, Mr.
Wheeler.

DARIUS WHEELER
Darius, please, and don't be kind. I'll just think you're feeling
sorry for me.

SETSUKO HEARN
No, but I did. Truly. It was very, I don't know, very sort of
Hunter S. Thompson meets Apocalypse Now. I mean that in
the best possible sense.

DARIUS WHEELER
Say no more, please. I think I get the picture. (*Handing*
SETSUKO HEARN *her drink*) Dozo.

SETSUKO HEARN
Thank you.

(*The sound of wooden clappers.*)

SETSUKO HEARN
(*Reapproaching the portrait.*)
This really is, it's exquisite. I'm guessing what? Kamakura period?

DARIUS WHEELER

Very good. Takanobu.

SETSUKO HEARN

Rings a bell.

DARIUS WHEELER

Portrait painter. Late twelfth century. Painted on silk. Japanese painting, up to that point, the human face, you know, it
was just a mask. A line here, a line there, two dots. Takanobu,
he was after this thing, to make something lifelike. To create
this thing that was real. Their eyes, everything that was going
on in their eyes. The way the light hits the skin. The shape of
the mouth. Kampai.

(DARIUS WHEELER *and* SETSUKO HEARN *drink. Light shift. The objects in*
WHEELER'*s loft space are revealed. Objects that look like works of art.*)

SETSUKO HEARN

It's good. Umeshu.

DARIUS WHEELER

Yes.

SETSUKO HEARN

Ume, it means summer plums. By themselves, they're bitter,
but once they've aged in the shochu, the spirits, they become
very sweet. It's really, it's lovely. Please, I don't want to keep
you from all your other guests.

DARIUS WHEELER

Don't worry. I don't know half the people out there. Trust me,
I won't be missed. So what did you think of the show tonight?
What do you think of Utagawa's work?

SETSUKO HEARN

I like it. I like the sensibility. I like the way he mixes Asian and
Western forms, the way he deploys classical techniques, and
yet his vision is so unconventional, so contemporary in a way—
I'm curious: how do you know Utagawa?

DARIUS WHEELER

I don't. I've never met the man. I'm hosting this little get-
together as a favor for an old friend.

SETSUKO HEARN

That's nice of you.

DARIUS WHEELER

I have my moments. He, like you, is quite a fan.

SETSUKO HEARN

And you are not.

DARIUS WHEELER

No.

SETSUKO HEARN

Not Oriental enough for you?

DARIUS WHEELER

It's just one white man's humble opinion.

SETSUKO HEARN

You're a traditionalist.

DARIUS WHEELER

Let's just say I have high standards.

(*The sound of wooden clappers.*)

SETSUKO HEARN
(*Approaching an art object.*)

Chinese?

DARIUS WHEELER

Liao Dynasty. The goddess Guanyin. That's an Undayana Buddha, eighth-century Korean, Silla Dynasty, gilt bronze. That's a, that's a Muromachi ink painting. Sixteenth century, Unkoku school, you can see what they call suiboku, or splashed ink technique, very unusual, very abstract. I got it at a private auction in Kyoto. No catalogue, no previewing, some of the stuff is in really bad shape, but every so often, you find a gem. I got it for a song. Do you like it?

SETSUKO HEARN

Very much.

DARIUS WHEELER

Here, wait, let me show you, I want to show you something else.

(DARIUS WHEELER *retrieves a jade figure from its case. The sound of the shakuhachi flute begins.*)

DARIUS WHEELER

Jade. Sung Dynasty era, over nine hundred years old. Very rare. Because the thing about jade, it's meant to be held, you see, and what it does, it warms to your skin, human touch, it alters the stone, there's a kind of chemical reaction, it actually changes the color of the stone. With each touch it changes over time, almost imperceptible, impossible to replicate. Very old jade like this, it comes in these translucent colors I can't describe, beautiful, unimaginably beautiful.

(DARIUS *holds out the jade figure.*)

Here. Feel.

(SETSUKO HEARN *touches the jade. Their hands touch.* DARIUS WHEELER *and* SETSUKO HEARN *begin to recede from view.*)

Scene 3

(*Light on* JOHN BELL. *The sound of the shakuhachi flute continues. As* JOHN BELL *speaks,* CLAIRE TSONG *is revealed. She's reading from a transcript.* JOHN BELL *is the voice behind the words she reads.*)

JOHN BELL

A list of beautiful things:
The curve of a lover's neck, delicate, white.
The touch of a lover's fingertips.
The weight of a lover's hair, the scent, clove and sandalwood.
The rustle of silk undone,
Warm breath against one's skin—

(*The sound of the shakuhachi flute ends.*)

Scene 4

(*A desk is revealed. The desk is covered with papers, catalogues, slides, pens, paints, paint brushes, books.* JOHN BELL *starts sifting through papers on the desk.* CLAIRE TSONG *approaches him. The sound of wooden clappers.*)

CLAIRE TSONG

John?

JOHN BELL

Claire? What are you doing here? You're not supposed to be here.

CLAIRE TSONG

Where's Utagawa?

JOHN BELL

I don't know, I don't know, I don't know where he is.

CLAIRE TSONG

Did you see him at the show?

JOHN BELL

No, he was running late. I got a message from his assistant. He was supposed to come directly here.

CLAIRE TSONG

Looking for something?

JOHN BELL

I wrote his assistant's number on this little piece of paper. I thought I left it here. Goddamnit.

CLAIRE TSONG
(Holding up the transcript.)
What's this?

JOHN BELL

Nothing.

CLAIRE TSONG

Where's it from?

JOHN BELL

Nowhere. *(Taking the transcript.)* Can you please not touch my stuff please, Claire, thank you.

CLAIRE TSONG

John—

JOHN BELL

I have to go.

CLAIRE TSONG

Oh come on, John. John—

(JOHN BELL *exits.* ELIZABETH NEWMAN-ORR *enters.*)

CLAIRE TSONG

Cheers.

ELIZABETH NEWMAN-ORR

It's so crowded out there. I needed some air. I was feeling a little flushed. Do you happen to know where Mr. Wheeler is by any chance?

CLAIRE TSONG

No clue.

ELIZABETH NEWMAN-ORR

I'm an old friend of his.

CLAIRE TSONG

He's got a lot of old friends. He's a very friendly guy. Make yourself at home. I'm sure he wouldn't mind.

ELIZABETH NEWMAN-ORR

Thanks.

(ELIZABETH NEWMAN-ORR *scans the works of art.*)

ELIZABETH NEWMAN-ORR

So what do you like?

(CLAIRE TSONG *studies the art objects, and then picks one.*)

CLAIRE TSONG

I like this. It's nice. A little showy, but nice.

ELIZABETH NEWMAN-ORR

Is it real?

CLAIRE TSONG

I guess it all depends on how you define real.

ELIZABETH NEWMAN-ORR

That's being a little coy, don't you think?

CLAIRE TSONG

It's old. It's painted by the guy it's supposed to be painted by. I guess that makes it real. Most of the time with a fake, it's pretty obvious. There's something really stupid going on, something that doesn't make sense. Wrong materials, shoddy workmanship.

ELIZABETH NEWMAN-ORR

And what is it you do? I don't think you said.

CLAIRE TSONG

I'm an artist actually. Mixed media.

ELIZABETH NEWMAN-ORR

That's a big, broad category. It could mean all kinds of things.

CLAIRE TSONG

Yes.

ELIZABETH NEWMAN-ORR
(*Referring to another art object:*)

Real?

CLAIRE TSONG

Iffy.

ELIZABETH NEWMAN-ORR

It looks real.

CLAIRE TSONG

Lots of things look real. You go to a museum, it all looks real.
And don't get me started on auction houses. What a shell
game those guys are running. You wouldn't believe the crap
that cycles through, third-rate counterfeits somebody paid a
lot of money for, and now they gotta pawn off on somebody
else, or else end up eating the loss.

ELIZABETH NEWMAN-ORR

You sound like an expert.

CLAIRE TSONG

It's not about expertise. It's all about the eye.

ELIZABETH NEWMAN-ORR

The eye? That sounds so hoodoo.

(*The sound of the shakuhachi flute begins. In the foreground,* SETSUKO
HEARN *and* DARIUS WHEELER *begin to come into view. They reconstruct
the pose that they were last in. The pose becomes real, fleshed out.*)

CLAIRE TSONG

It's like it's physical, you know, I'm talking about a physical
sensation, an instinct. It's like there's an invisible thread between you and this thing—I don't know. It's hard to explain,
it's not objective, it's irrational, it's completely irrational. You
can't quantify or predict it. You just know, all of a sudden you
know.

(*The sound of wooden clappers.*)

Scene 5

(The sound of the shakuhachi flute continues. JOHN BELL *and* OWEN MATTHIASSEN *appear.* JOHN BELL, OWEN MATTHIASSEN, CLAIRE TSONG, ELIZABETH NEWMAN-ORR, DARIUS WHEELER, *and* SETSUKO HEARN *are figures in a woodblock print, flesh figures in a floating world. The sound of wooden clappers.* DARIUS WHEELER *and* CLAIRE TSONG *see each other. It's a moment of nagashime, a sideways glance as seen in old woodblock prints of kabuki actors. The sound of wooden clappers. The sound of the shakuhachi flute ends.)*

Scene 6

(The woodblock print instantly dissolves into movement. CLAIRE TSONG, ELIZABETH NEWMAN-ORR, *and* JOHN BELL *exit in different directions. The sound of a party in progress.)*

OWEN MATTHIASSEN

Darius—

DARIUS WHEELER

Owen—

SETSUKO HEARN

Dr. Matthiassen—

OWEN MATTHIASSEN

Setsuko, my dear, I'm so glad you made it. Utagawa should be here any minute now. Darius, what are you drinking?

DARIUS WHEELER

Plum wine.

OWEN MATTHIASSEN

Umeshu, how delightful.

DARIUS WHEELER

You're in fine spirits, Owen.

OWEN MATTHIASSEN

I am, I am. I'll have a drop, if it's not too much of a bother.

DARIUS WHEELER

Not at all.

(DARIUS WHEELER *prepares a drink.*)

OWEN MATTHIASSEN

Darius, you've outdone yourself. I just ran into an old friend
of mine from Waseda I haven't seen in ages, and some woman
from the consulate, turns out I knew her father. I see you've
met my brilliant young colleague.

DARIUS WHEELER

I have. I had no idea.

SETSUKO HEARN

Dr. Matthiassen is too kind.

OWEN MATTHIASSEN

Dr. Hearn is a shining star in our department. We're incredibly lucky to have her join our ranks. Almost lost her to Stan-
ford, you know.

SETSUKO HEARN

You are really, really too kind.

(DARIUS WHEELER *gives* OWEN MATTHIASSEN *his drink.*)

OWEN MATTHIASSEN

What happened to your hand?

DARIUS WHEELER

Nothing.

OWEN MATTHIASSEN

Darius, you're hemorrhaging.

DARIUS WHEELER

I'm fine, Owen, I'm fine. (*To* SETSUKO HEARN) So what are
you working on exactly?

OWEN MATTHIASSEN

Dr. Hearn's field of expertise is writing from the eleventh century, diaries, memoirs, pillow books written by women of the
Heian era. How the writer speaks in her most private moments, depictions of her interior life, the private self.

DARIUS WHEELER

That doesn't sound humdrum at all.

(SETSUKO HEARN *turns away, approaching an art object.*)

OWEN MATTHIASSEN

Humdrum? Hardly. Where did you get that idea? On the contrary, it's fascinating, the feminine vernacular in the golden age of Japanese literature. Some wonderful women writing back then: Sei Shonagon, Izumi Shikibu—

DARIUS WHEELER

Lady Murasaki.

SETSUKO HEARN

Very good.

OWEN MATTHIASSEN

The Tale of Genji. Darius, I'm impressed. Have you read it?

DARIUS WHEELER

I have not.

OWEN MATTHIASSEN

Oh, but you must.

SETSUKO HEARN

You'd like it.

DARIUS WHEELER

Would I?

OWEN MATTHIASSEN

It's very engaging. Romance, intrigue. Some fine translations out there, Waley's always good, accessible, surprisingly modern, I find.

DARIUS WHEELER

Owen, I haven't read a book in over a decade.

OWEN MATTHIASSEN

Nonsense.

DARIUS WHEELER

Sad, but true. I'm a philistine, Owen. You've just always been too polite to notice. I had no idea I was conversing with such a shining star. I have to say, I feel a little out of my depth in such learned company.

OWEN MATTHIASSEN

Oh you do not. Don't listen to a word he says. (*Joining* SETSUKO HEARN) Breathtaking, isn't it? Nobody has this kind of stuff anymore. I don't know how he does it. Fantastic pieces, uncanny really. Good eye. I have to say, I take a little pride in my contribution to all of it. I've known Darius for ages, you know.

SETSUKO HEARN

You studied with Dr. Matthiassen?

OWEN MATTHIASSEN

Oh no no no. Darius has never been much for the academic life, I'm afraid.

DARIUS WHEELER

I was a lazy bum, dropped out of school, never made it through my second year.

SETSUKO HEARN

It doesn't seem to have held you back.

OWEN MATTHIASSEN

An understatement, my dear, you have no idea. He's done fabulously well. I always knew he would.

DARIUS WHEELER

Owen is an eternal optimist.

OWEN MATTHIASSEN

I'm a fantastic judge of human nature. The man leads a charmed life. I envy you, Darius, I do, surrounded by things most of us only see in picture books. A nice life. I could think of a lot worse. You have an eye for beautiful things.

DARIUS WHEELER

I like to think so.

SETSUKO HEARN

You don't care for Utagawa's work, however.

OWEN MATTHIASSEN

Darius despises contemporary art. He's very contrary, willfully anachronistic.

DARIUS WHEELER

I like his shunga.

OWEN MATTHIASSEN

Ah, yes, his erotic prints.

SETSUKO HEARN

And why is that?

OWEN MATTHIASSEN

They're very, very vulgar.

DARIUS WHEELER

Exactly. They're honest. They're getting at something basic and real.

OWEN MATTHIASSEN

The more graphic, the less beautiful, I find.

DARIUS WHEELER

I don't think Utagawa's about beauty, Owen. I think that's precisely the problem. I think he's about making a point. He's about ideas, his art is all about ideas, ideas about ideas.

(*Enter* JOHN BELL.)

OWEN MATTHIASSEN

I disagree entirely.

JOHN BELL

Mr. Wheeler—

DARIUS WHEELER

It's just a series of abstractions tarted up to look like art.

OWEN MATTHIASSEN

I disagree, I have to disagree.

JOHN BELL

Mr. Wheeler—

DARIUS WHEELER

I mean the guy's got craft, I'll give him that. Technically, he's great, but what he has to say—I wonder why it is that he can't just make a beautiful thing and leave it at that.

SETSUKO HEARN

I wonder what you mean when you say beautiful.

DARIUS WHEELER

Beautiful means beautiful.

SETSUKO HEARN

That's something of a dead end, don't you think?

DARIUS WHEELER

No, no I don't.

SETSUKO HEARN

It's so absolute.

DARIUS WHEELER

Of course, it is. It has to be. What are you left with otherwise?

(*The sound of wooden clappers.*)

JOHN BELL

Mr. Wheeler—

DARIUS WHEELER

I'm sorry—John, what is it?

JOHN BELL

I just spoke with Utagawa san's assistant just now, and it seems—well, it seems that he won't be able to make it this evening.

OWEN MATTHIASSEN

What do you mean? I spoke to his assistant on the phone just this afternoon.

JOHN BELL

Something came up apparently, some sudden obligation he couldn't get out of. He sends his sincere regrets.

OWEN MATTHIASSEN

I see. How disappointing. I was so looking forward to meeting the man in person. Although I guess I shouldn't be surprised. I hear he's somewhat of a recluse, you know. Poor Darius, putting this whole evening together, loathe his work as you do. We should tell the other guests.

DARIUS WHEELER

I'll take care of it.

OWEN MATTHIASSEN

Well, there's nothing to be done. Another time perhaps. Life is full of the unexpected, best to be flexible, I find. At any rate, what a delight, my dear, to find you here. Here, let's go this way. I want you to see this, mandala painting, Nepalese,

thirteenth century, when I first saw the thing, I was completely
stupefied . . .

(OWEN MATTHIASSEN *and* SETSUKO HEARN *exit.* DARIUS WHEELER *and*
JOHN BELL *remain. The sound of wooden clappers.*)

Scene 7

(*The party begins to dissolve. Guests begin to exit into the night.* DARIUS
WHEELER *begins to exit after* OWEN MATTHIASSEN *and* SETSUKO HEARN.
Enter ELIZABETH NEWMAN-ORR.)

DARIUS WHEELER

All right, let's wind this up, shall we. John, can you make an
announcement: The guest of honor is a no-show. Everybody
just go home.

JOHN BELL

Mr. Wheeler, one more thing.

DARIUS WHEELER

Yeah, John, what? What is it?

ELIZABETH NEWMAN-ORR

Mr. Wheeler, Elizabeth Newman-Orr. It's a pleasure. You have
a beautiful space here, so many beautiful things.

DARIUS WHEELER

Thank you. Do I know you?

ELIZABETH NEWMAN-ORR

I'm a friend of Utagawa's. I'm actually, I'm more of a friend of
a friend, really an acquaintance, I'm more of an acquaintance.

DARIUS WHEELER

I see.

ELIZABETH NEWMAN-ORR

I lie.

DARIUS WHEELER

I see.

ELIZABETH NEWMAN-ORR
I'm uninvited. I know no one. You've found me out, I'm afraid.

DARIUS WHEELER
I won't tell. Now if you'll excuse me.

ELIZABETH NEWMAN-ORR
Mr. Wheeler, if I could, I was speaking just now with your assistant. I was hoping you and I could find a time to meet, tomorrow perhaps. I have a small matter I was hoping to discuss
with you.

DARIUS WHEELER
Tomorrow's kinda tight for me.

ELIZABETH NEWMAN-ORR
I believe you'll find it worth your while.

DARIUS WHEELER
And should I trust your judgment?

ELIZABETH NEWMAN-ORR
I'm a woman of unerring judgment.

DARIUS WHEELER
I'm intrigued. Should I be intrigued?

ELIZABETH NEWMAN-ORR
I think so. I'll be glad to explain everything at length. Tomorrow perhaps?

DARIUS WHEELER
So eager. All right, look, why don't you set something up with
John. Now if you'll excuse me.

ELIZABETH NEWMAN-ORR
Of course. Good night, Mr. Wheeler.

(ELIZABETH NEWMAN-ORR *and* JOHN BELL *exit. The sound of a party
breaking up. Kurogo, stage assistants in black overcostumes, remove props
and scenery. The sound of wooden clappers.* OWEN MATTHIASSEN *appears
holding a portfolio.*)

OWEN MATTHIASSEN
Darius, a word with you.

Scene 8

(*Light shift. Late evening.* OWEN MATTHIASSEN *and* DARIUS WHEELER *occupy a sliver of light.*)

DARIUS WHEELER

Where did Dr. Hearn go?

OWEN MATTHIASSEN

She had to leave, the lateness of the hour.

DARIUS WHEELER

What a pity.

OWEN MATTHIASSEN

She said to tell you that she had a lovely time. Marvelous girl, isn't she. Very smart, humbling really, and so young. My God, I remember being that young. I remember it vividly. How did I get to be so old?

DARIUS WHEELER

You're not that old.

OWEN MATTHIASSEN

I'm ancient. It's ridiculous.

DARIUS WHEELER

You're young at heart.

OWEN MATTHIASSEN

Don't condescend, Darius. It's not nice.

DARIUS WHEELER

What do you have there, Owen? One of Utagawa's sly little "masterpieces"?

OWEN MATTHIASSEN

Out of my price range, I'm afraid. No no, something else. Very exciting. More to your taste, I assure you. Here take a look. Stumbled upon it today, private gallery, little hole in the wall, one of those things, at the right place, at the right time.

(*A woodblock print is revealed. A reproduction of a woodblock print. Larger than life.* OWEN MATTHIASSEN *and* DARIUS WHEELER *appear as tiny human figures in the foreground of Hokusai's landscape.*)

OWEN MATTHIASSEN

Hokusai for Chrissakes. When I first saw it, I couldn't believe my eyes. Fuji from Kajikazawa. First edition, not cheap, but fair, more than fair, and all things considered, in pretty good shape, some water damage, it's true, and the color's faded a bit, but other than that—I mean, good Lord, almost two hundred years old. Paper. Can you imagine. It's a miracle it hasn't sustained worse damage. Survival is a kind of beautiful thing, isn't it. After all these years. Look at the mountain through the mist. Gorgeous, just gorgeous.

DARIUS WHEELER

Owen, this is a fake.

OWEN MATTHIASSEN

What are you talking about?

DARIUS WHEELER

It's good. I mean, whoever did this is pretty good.

OWEN MATTHIASSEN

Well, I know you're the expert, but I like to think I know a thing or two. For God's sakes, I've been collecting prints for years. Look at the water marks, the publisher's seal. The artist's hand is proof enough, the vigor and delicacy of the lines, the weight of detail. I'm telling you, I've examined this print. I've studied it. I know what it looks like. I know what it should look like.

DARIUS WHEELER

It's nice, Owen.

OWEN MATTHIASSEN

Nice? It's not just nice. It's spot on.

DARIUS WHEELER

Whoever the artist is, he knows what he's doing. The only problem is: whoever he is, he's not Hokusai. Look at the color. Look at it, really look.

(*The colors of the woodblock print slowly transform, becoming unnaturally bright and lurid.*)

DARIUS WHEELER

The color is a dead giveaway. It's all wrong. I don't care how much you distress it, underneath the stain, whatever this is, tea, coffee grounds, ash, it's way too bright, way too brassy. Look at these blues. Aniline pigment, artificial, inorganic, imported to Japan from Germany. This print dates—or should date—from the1830s. This kind of pigment wasn't introduced into Japan until the mid-1850s. We're talking twenty years after the fact. The print's nice, Owen. It just happens to be fake.

(OWEN MATTHIASSEN *fades away. The sound of wooden clappers. Light on* CLAIRE TSONG *in a distant corner of the space.*)

Scene 9

(*A disclaimer in fine print.*)

CLAIRE TSONG

The vendor will not be responsible for the correctness of description, authenticity, or any defect or fault in or concerning any article, and makes no warranty whatever, but will sell each object exactly as is, without recourse.

(*The sound of wooden clappers.*)

CLAIRE TSONG

Always read the fine print. There is always fine print.

(*The sound of the shakuhachi flute.* CLAIRE TSONG *and the woodblock print fade away.* DARIUS WHEELER *remains.*)

Scene 10

(*Pre-dawn light. The sound of the shakuhachi flute continues. A Kurogo, a stage assistant, enters. His face is wrapped in black fabric. He carries a large rectangular panel covered by a drop cloth. He removes the cloth, revealing an Edo period screen. On the screen is a painting of a garden in autumn.*)

(*The sound of wooden clappers.*)

(*The Kurogo begins removing his black over-costume.* DARIUS WHEELER *goes to the desk, and notices the transcript* CLAIRE TSONG *was looking through earlier. He picks it up and reads.* SETSUKO HEARN *is revealed in a sliver of light.*)

SETSUKO HEARN
A list of beautiful things:
The curve of a lover's neck,
The touch of a lover's fingertips,
The weight of a lover's hair, the scent,
The rustle of silk undone,
Your tongue, your lips,
The taste, salt and wet,
Warm breath against one's skin.

(*The Kurogo removes the last piece of fabric covering his face. The Kurogo is revealed to be* JOHN BELL. *The sound of wooden clappers. The sound of the shakuhachi flute ends.* SETSUKO HEARN *vanishes.* DARIUS WHEELER *exits.*)

Scene 11

(*The day after the party. Mid-morning.* WHEELER's *loft space.* JOHN BELL *is examining the screen that he unwrapped in the previous scene.* CLAIRE TSONG *is packing up, putting away the dropcloth along with various paints and tools.*)

CLAIRE TSONG

All right, you're not listening, or maybe I'm not making myself clear. All this, at the end of the day, is fine furnishing, bric-a-brac for the leisure class.

JOHN BELL

Last I looked, Claire, it was called art.

CLAIRE TSONG

I'm telling you, pal, it's all just capital.

JOHN BELL

Spare me, please.

CLAIRE TSONG

OK, you know what your problem is? You romanticize this stuff. You spend all your time surrounded by all this "art," and it's affecting your brain. Strip it all away, and all you have is money jazzed up to make you think it's something more than money—which it's not. That it has some kind of deep, spiritual aura because it's "art"—which it doesn't.

JOHN BELL

I know you don't believe that.

CLAIRE TSONG

I believe all kinds of things.

(*The sound of wooden clappers.*)

CLAIRE TSONG

So? What do you think? How does it look?

JOHN BELL

It's nice, Claire. This is really nice work.

CLAIRE TSONG

Is this a surprise?

JOHN BELL

What do you want me to say?

CLAIRE TSONG

That I'm brilliant, a genius, the best.

JOHN BELL

You're brilliant, a genius, the best.

CLAIRE TSONG

Fuck you.

JOHN BELL

You are, Claire. The restorations are really, they're great. I know what this looked like before.

CLAIRE TSONG

Trashed. A lost cause.

JOHN BELL

Pretty much.

(JOHN BELL *cuts* CLAIRE *a check.*)

JOHN BELL

Listen, Wheeler has some other screens he'd like you to take a look at. Minor stuff: mildew damage, fading, standard wear and tear.

CLAIRE TSONG

Wheeler can kiss my ass. Like I sit around waiting for him to kick down some crap for me to tinker with. Like I don't have better things to do.

JOHN BELL

Claire, it's way too early in the day.

CLAIRE TSONG

I don't even know why you still work for that guy. He's like the evil empire.

JOHN BELL

You work for him, too.

CLAIRE TSONG

I'm an independent contractor. There's a difference. I'm my own little business of which I am the boss. I do the work because I choose to.

JOHN BELL

Why? I mean, why do you choose to work for Wheeler?

CLAIRE TSONG
(*Taking the check*)

Imp of the perverse. I don't know. Who knows. I'm a masochist, I guess. Besides I'm subsidizing my own art— Look, don't change the subject. I'm trying to educate you. Somebody has to. This is about your future. These are economic realities I'm talking about.

(CLAIRE TSONG *retrieves a can of spray paint. She begins to shake it.*)

CLAIRE TSONG

How much does Wheeler pay you, if you don't mind me asking.

JOHN BELL

I don't like talking about money, Claire.

CLAIRE TSONG

Why?

JOHN BELL

It makes me feel awkward.

CLAIRE TSONG

Guilty?

JOHN BELL

No. I don't know. Maybe a little. I don't know.

CLAIRE TSONG

You act like it's a dirty word, and it's not. It's just a thing like any other thing. Don't mystify it. Don't do that to yourself. You should've quit a long time ago. It's so stupid. It doesn't make any sense.

(CLAIRE TSONG *aims the spray paint can at the screen she just restored.*)

JOHN BELL

Claire—

CLAIRE TSONG

Would I be destroying it?

JOHN BELL

Claire—

CLAIRE TSONG

Or restoring it? How would I be affecting its market value? But now here's the thing: what if I happened to make it a better painting? Or better yet, what if you couldn't tell the difference?

JOHN BELL

Claire, please—

CLAIRE TSONG

Do you really want to spend the rest of your life worrying

about market value? Because frankly, I think you're a lot more interesting than that.

JOHN BELL

Wait—

(CLAIRE TSONG *sprays.* JOHN BELL *blocks the screen with his body. A flower of paint blooms on his shirt.*)

CLAIRE TSONG

You're brilliant, for one thing. It's like your brain is a very big thing, and it's filled with all this knowledge. You try to hide it, but I'm so onto your game. You know all this stuff, you don't even let on the half of it.

JOHN BELL

Yeah? What stuff do I know?

CLAIRE TSONG

Art, for one. Literature. Languages, you're like fluent in all these languages. What do you speak? No, wait, let me guess: Japanese. Uh huh. Korean? Right. Chinese— how many dialects? No, wait, let me: Mandarin, Hunan, Cantonese—

JOHN BELL

My Cantonese is really, really basic.

CLAIRE TSONG

Oh my God, John, stop it. You're learned. Step to it, buddy, you're really learned.

JOHN BELL

I have a masters in East Asian studies and an unfinished thesis that's never going to get finished. I happen to know a few languages. I also happen to have a drawerful of unfinished novels, and once upon a time, a long time ago, I played the French horn.

CLAIRE TSONG

You're a Renaissance man.

JOHN BELL

Jack of all trades, master of none.

CLAIRE TSONG

John, honey, you gotta work on your self-esteem. You're withering on the vine here. Wheeler's using you. Cheap, over-educated labor. What are you anyway?

JOHN BELL

What am I? I don't know, Claire. That's so existential.

CLAIRE TSONG

What's your title?

JOHN BELL

I'm an assistant.

CLAIRE TSONG

And what does that mean exactly?

JOHN BELL

Uh, that I assist. Look, Claire, I like my job. And I like Wheeler.

(*Enter* DARIUS WHEELER.)

JOHN BELL

The guy's like a legend, broke all the rules, and I guess I kinda respect that.

CLAIRE TSONG

Please. Dealers are the scum of the earth, and Wheeler's in a class all his own.

JOHN BELL

He's complex.

CLAIRE TSONG

He's a prick.

JOHN BELL

He's a complicated guy.

CLAIRE TSONG

He's a self-absorbed, narcissistic prick. He's also a liar, a con artist, and a thief.

(*Enter* ELIZABETH NEWMAN-ORR. *The sound of wooden clappers.*)

DARIUS WHEELER

I was at this party once in Boston, and this attractive Asian woman comes up to me from out of nowhere, and she just starts in on me—calls me a liar, a con artist, and a few other choice names I'm not going to share in mixed company, and people, you know, they're starting to turn around and look, and before I know it, right, she's hurling her drink at me, hard, you know, in my face, and I hear the glass shatter, and the room goes silent, and I feel a heat and a kind of stinging, and I reach up and touch my face, and I look at my hand, and I see there's this red liquid all over my fingers, and I'm thinking to myself, Jesus Christ, I'm bleeding. Turned out to be tomato juice. But for a second or two, I thought it was blood.

(*The sound of wooden clappers.* JOHN BELL *and* CLAIRE TSONG *exit.*)

Scene 12

(*Late morning.* DARIUS WHEELER, *and* ELIZABETH NEWMAN-ORR *remain.*)

DARIUS WHEELER

The world is full of crackpots. Most of them are harmless, but then again you never know.

ELIZABETH NEWMAN-ORR

So what was the story? Who was she?

DARIUS WHEELER

Who knows. A kook.

ELIZABETH NEWMAN-ORR

Your reputation, I have to say, precedes you.

DARIUS WHEELER

And what exactly have you heard?

ELIZABETH NEWMAN-ORR

Nothing but praise.

DARIUS WHEELER

Is that right?

ELIZABETH NEWMAN-ORR

Praise tempered by maybe just a little bit of envy.

DARIUS WHEELER

Look, I don't need to tell you, this business is full of thwarted souls with nothing good to say about anyone. I'm a lucky man. Some people have a problem with that. Don't get me wrong, I'm good at what I do, but I'm also very lucky. That's all it really is, you know. Dumb luck.

ELIZABETH NEWMAN-ORR

That's very modest of you.

DARIUS WHEELER

It's the God's honest truth.

ELIZABETH NEWMAN-ORR

How homespun.

(ELIZABETH NEWMAN-ORR *moves toward the screen from the previous scene, the screen that* CLAIRE TSONG *restored*.)

ELIZABETH NEWMAN-ORR

This is new.

DARIUS WHEELER

It's a beauty, isn't it? Just came in this morning. Edo era. Museum quality, in mint condition.

ELIZABETH NEWMAN-ORR

What kind of restorations?

DARIUS WHEELER

Hardly any at all.

(*The sound of wooden clappers.*)

DARIUS WHEELER

Interested?

ELIZABETH NEWMAN-ORR

Another time perhaps.

DARIUS WHEELER

By then it'll be gone. It never pays to wait. It's the nature of the business. Things move, they get traded, they circulate.

ELIZABETH NEWMAN-ORR

I guess I'll just have to take my chances. I'm curious: do you ever find yourself getting attached to a particular object, something very special?

DARIUS WHEELER

Rarely.

ELIZABETH NEWMAN-ORR

I would find that hard, I think.

DARIUS WHEELER

Things come and go in this life. It's best not to get too attached.

ELIZABETH NEWMAN-ORR

That's very Zen of you.

DARIUS WHEELER

What can I say? I'm a Zen kinda guy. Now what can I do for you today?

ELIZABETH NEWMAN-ORR

Suppose there were a painting, very ancient, very rare, part of a large, private collection in Hong Kong. A Taiwanese banker and his Austrian wife.

DARIUS WHEELER

Villa on Lugard Road. A smallish collection, some nice lacquerware, Imari, tasteful, very tasteful.

ELIZABETH NEWMAN-ORR

Keeping track of the bodies?

DARIUS WHEELER

I'm a dealer, Ms. Orr. You never know when someone's going to want to sell.

ELIZABETH NEWMAN-ORR

You know the painting I'm talking about.

DARIUS WHEELER

I might.

ELIZABETH NEWMAN-ORR

Suppose my clients purchased this painting in a private sale, and it turned out, unbeknownst to either seller or purchaser, that the painting was a national treasure.

DARIUS WHEELER

Ah.

ELIZABETH NEWMAN-ORR

If authorities were to get wind of the transaction, which they would, if we were to go through more traditional channels of sale and transfer, the painting would need to be returned to its country of origin.

DARIUS WHEELER

It's tricky these days.

ELIZABETH NEWMAN-ORR

I was given your name.

DARIUS WHEELER

Given my name by whom?

ELIZABETH NEWMAN-ORR

I'd rather not say.

DARIUS WHEELER

Ever mysterious. I like that quality in a woman. In a business associate, I like it less so. Now if you'll excuse me.

ELIZABETH NEWMAN-ORR

Can't we be candid with one another, Mr. Wheeler? I'd like that so much. It would make everything so much easier.

DARIUS WHEELER

What are we talking about?

ELIZABETH NEWMAN-ORR

I think you have an idea.

DARIUS WHEELER

Why don't you spell it out for me.

ELIZABETH NEWMAN-ORR

The discreet transport of an object from one place to another.

(The sound of wooden clappers.)

DARIUS WHEELER

Ah. I see. Well, now, OK this is the thing, Ms. Orr, about the part of the world we're dealing with here, because it's all a little cowboys and Indians, and that can go a lot of ways. You're talking tariffs and tea money, never mind some government type getting a bug up his ass, and throwing a wrench in the works. Now it used to be, you could go in, pick up almost anything. Nowadays, it's a different story. These people, they've gotten very touchy about their culture. They see us raiding their temples, pilfering their

Buddhas, and they get a little pissed off, understandably perhaps, and they confiscate our property, and more than that, they throw people like myself in jail for long and indeterminate prison sentences— Have you ever spent time in a third-world jail, Ms. Orr?

ELIZABETH NEWMAN-ORR
Ten percent of the purchase price placed in an off-shore account.

DARIUS WHEELER
You have got to be kidding me.

ELIZABETH NEWMAN-ORR
Fifteen percent.

DARIUS WHEELER
Twenty percent. Half up front, half upon the object's arrival.

ELIZABETH NEWMAN-ORR
I think—I think that can be arranged.

(ELIZABETH NEWMAN-ORR *exits.*)

Scene 13

(*The sound of the shakuhachi flute begins.* DARIUS WHEELER *returns to his desk, and picks up the transcript he was reading earlier. He scans the pages.* SETSUKO HEARN *appears in a sliver of light. As she speaks, she becomes more visible, more real.*)

SETSUKO HEARN
No rain tonight, no moon, the air is perfectly still
Not even the faintest breeze stirs the leaves.
In the pool in the garden below, carp swim beneath the surface—
Flashes of white in the murky green
Their bellies slick and wet—
The tickle of waterweed
The soft wet moss—
The curve of your neck, your fingertips
The rustle of silk undone—
Your mouth, your tongue
Your lips, the taste of your lips, salt, wet

The warmth of your breath against my skin
And I am seized with sudden longing.

(*The sound of woodern clappers. The sound of the shakuhachi flute ends.* SETSUKO HEARN *vanishes.*)

Scene 14

(*Enter* JOHN BELL *carrying files.*)

DARIUS WHEELER

John?

JOHN BELL

Yes?

DARIUS WHEELER

What's this?

JOHN BELL

What's what?

DARIUS WHEELER
(*Holding up the transcript:*)
This. What's this?

JOHN BELL

Oh. That. It's a, it's a—

(*The sound of wooden clappers.*)

Scene 15

(*A history of origins.*)

JOHN BELL

It's a transcription—

Of a manuscript.

It turned up in a private library, and was sent to us for appraisal just the other day.

I've been meaning to tell you—

I've been translating it, looking into its provenance.

Japanese, eleventh century

Heian era—

A memoir or pillow book.

The author remains nameless, hard biographical data is, as is often the case, scant.

The earliest known owner of the document appears to have been a Dutch trader and sometime scholar by the name of Van Rijn, stationed on the island of Dejima in the seventeenth century.

There's an oblique mention of it in a letter he wrote to his wife. (I have it on file.) How or why he disposed of it remains unclear. Regardless of the disposition, the document disappears for almost a century, resurfacing again in the first decade of the eighteenth century, when it was transferred along with various other scrolls—

To a money lender in Edo—

Whose eldest son lost it one night in a single game of chance, to an affluent sake maker by the name of Sato. (I found a reference in an article on the redistribution of capital in the Edo period by a French Marxist in the Sixties, his name escapes me.) Sato presented the document shortly thereafter to the celebrated courtesan Hanaogi, who kept it until her death, when it was appropriated by the proprietor of a local tea house in satisfaction of outstanding and unspecified debts.

Next we hear of it, it's in the possession of one Constance Hooley, the daughter of Methodist missionaries from Buffalo, New York, transplanted to Japan in the 1880s to spread the word of the Lord— She makes passing mention of it in a small, self-published anthology of Japanese literature compiled by her on behalf of her ladies' church group.

Upon the Reverend Hooley's death, Constance Hooley sells the document, along with various other Asian antiquities, to a

Chinese shipping magnate by the name of Liu, who sells it shortly thereafter to a wealthy Englishman and amateur poet, one Thaddeus Biddle, who happened to be touring the Orient on holiday, in search of souvenirs. Biddle pays an astronomical price by the standards of the day—he was, he writes, "utterly enchanted by the work, besotted by its curious and ineffable beauty." (I'm quoting directly from his journal here.) He took the document along with the rest of his acquisitions back to Europe, where it eventually ended up in the hands of an antiquarian in Lyon who bought it in the years preceding World War One, and sold it to a Scotsman in the spring of nineteen fifty-two, who bequeathed it to his nephew along with the rest of his private library in the fall of nineteen seventy-nine.

There is a bill of sale. The original's in pretty bad shape.

That's about the long and the short of it.

I don't know the whole story. I just translated it, that's all.

DARIUS WHEELER

Heian era?

JOHN BELL

Yes. A memoir of sorts. It actually partakes more of the zuihitsu genre, loosely translated: books of miscellany. A hybrid form consisting of lists, poems, memoir fragments, and observations. A pillow book, if you will.

DARIUS WHEELER

What do you make of it? Is it authentic?

JOHN BELL

From what I can tell, it appears to be, yes.

(DARIUS WHEELER *exits with the transcript.*)

JOHN BELL

Mr. Wheeler, wait—

(*The sound of wooden clappers.* CLAIRE TSONG *appears.*)

CLAIRE TSONG

So what exactly did you tell him?

(*The sound of wooden clappers.*)

Scene 16

(*Late afternoon of the same day.* WHEELER's *loft.*)

JOHN BELL

I lied. Claire, I lied. I can't believe this. What have I done? What was I thinking? I don't know what came over me. I was totally caught up in something else. I wasn't thinking. He caught me completely off guard. I panicked. I made up this stupid story right on the spot. It was like a reflex. It was like it wasn't even me doing the talking.

CLAIRE TSONG

And Wheeler?

JOHN BELL

He believed me. He believed every word out of my mouth.

CLAIRE TSONG

Wow. That is so—great.

JOHN BELL

What are you? Nuts? Don't you get it? I lied not just once or twice, but over and over and over again, and the thing is, I didn't even mean to do it, even as I was looking this guy right in the eye, this guy I look up to, this guy I like— I know you don't like him, but I do, I like the guy, Claire —and I'm telling him all these facts, except they're not facts, because I'm lying through my teeth, I just happen to be lying with this incredible degree of specificity. I don't know what came over me. This is so unethical. Not to mention illegal.

CLAIRE TSONG

Fraud.

JOHN BELL

Jesus Christ.

CLAIRE TSONG

Look, it's only illegal if he tries to sell it.

JOHN BELL

Oh my God, what have I done? Claire, what have I done? I can't believe this.

CLAIRE TSONG

How was it written?

(*The sound of wooden clappers.*)

CLAIRE TSONG

I mean, I know it's a "translation," but your original, was it written in kanji or kana or what?

JOHN BELL

Kana, it was written in kana. Or more accurately speaking, onna moji, which is a kind of, it's a kind of, it's a kind of precursor to hiragana. Syllabic, purely syllabic.

CLAIRE TSONG

How close to contemporary Japanese?

JOHN BELL

There are, you know, there are echoes. I mean, the meanings of individual words have changed over time, and the usages, how the language sounds, the spoken language, and the syntax, the syntax is different, archaic, it's archaic, but the strokes, the strokes are pretty much the same, I mean the basic shape is identical, I mean virtually identical, I mean I guess it depends on how you define identical.

CLAIRE TSONG
(*Handing* JOHN BELL *a paintbrush*)

Here.

(*The sound of wooden clappers.*)

CLAIRE TSONG

Show me.

(*The sound of the shakuhachi flute.* JOHN BELL *draws Japanese kana with the paintbrush on a panel of the shoji screen. He writes* きれい. *He returns the paintbrush to* CLAIRE TSONG. *She mimics his strokes, and picks up where he left off. She continues to write. She creates the artifact. Darkness.*)

Scene 17

(*A translation. Japanese lettering etches itself into the void, strokes of ink on blank pages. The sound of the shakuhachi flute.* SETSUKO HEARN *appears in a sliver of light dressed as the Heian era lady. As she speaks,* DARIUS WHEELER *emerges from the darkness.* JOHN BELL *and* CLAIRE TSONG *create the pillow book.*)

SETSUKO HEARN

In the evening, I hear a tapping at my screen, like the sound of rain on the eaves, and yet there is no rain tonight. There is no moon. The air is perfectly still. Within my chambers, the air is dark as ink. I cannot see your face. In the pool in the garden below, carp swim beneath the water, their bellies brush against the cool wet mud. I hear them breathing in the dark.

JOHN BELL

A list of beautiful things:
The touch of a lover's fingertips.
The rustle of silk undone—

SETSUKO HEARN

Your mouth, your tongue,
The hollow of my neck,
The inside of my thigh,
The taste, salt and wet,
Warm breath against one's skin—

(*The sound of the shakuhachi flute changes tone. Light on the screen that* CLAIRE TSONG *restored. A painting of a garden. It is an autumn scene: bare branches shrouded in mist. The painting of the garden in autumn begins to transform into a painting of a garden in summer: branches in bloom, ripe fruit. Fireflies. A summer night.*)

DARIUS WHEELER

I hear the ladies whispering of late. So many tongues fluttering all at once. It's as though I live in a nest of starlings. If I could, I would snip each wagging tongue, chop it into little bits, and feed the bits to the carp.

CLAIRE TSONG

A secret no longer secret is like an oyster pried open.
How clumsy the blade, how strange the pearl.

SETSUKO HEARN

I have taken a new lover who is not without charms. Lord S
wonders why I am otherwise engaged this evening. I tell him
I am busy chanting sutras.

JOHN BELL

A list of unsuitable things: Gossip, slander, accusation.

DARIUS WHEELER

I hear things, Lord S says. Do you? Rumors, he says. Do not
take me for a fool.

JOHN BELL

Do not tramp filth into my chambers. Lord S asks if I am
seeing another. Bad enough that he suspects and that I lie.
Worse that I do not care.

SETSUKO HEARN

At night, my new lover whispers monstrous things to me, too
terrifying to imagine. I feel a tingling through my belly, a chill
more pleasurable than words.

DARIUS WHEELER

Who is this new lover?

CLAIRE TSONG

She is a lady of the fifth rank, new to court. I spied her at the
moon-viewing, her sleeve spilled over the edge of her vessel,
and trailed across the water—crimson, vermilion, a sliver of
white.

SETSUKO HEARN

Her skill with silk, I have found, is surpassed only by her skill
in love. She is very skillful in love.

DARIUS WHEELER

Why do you tell me these things.

SETSUKO HEARN

Why? I do not know. Faithless, I am a faithless creature. I received the letter in the morning on violet paper bound with
plumeria. So exquisite I could not bear to open it.

(The sound of shakuhachi flute changes tone. OWEN MATTHAISSEN *and*
ELIZABETH NEWMAN-ORR *become visible in slivers of light.)*

ELIZABETH NEWMAN-ORR
On the fifteenth day of the eighth month, we catch fireflies in
the sleeves of our robes. They glitter through the summer silk.
Later, we play games of chance.

OWEN MATTHIASSEN
A visiting sage entertains us with his parrot, a strange green bird
who utters bits of wisdom. Lord S drinks too much rice wine,
and comports himself poorly. His wife sends a reproachful note
the following morning. Her handwriting, I notice, is very poor.

SETSUKO HEARN
Some women are wives and mothers, I tell him. Some women
choose different, less familiar paths. He calls on me several
times afterwards. His letters moulder at my door.

DARIUS WHEELER
A list of unsuitable things:

ELIZABETH NEWMAN-ORR
A certain powerful man whose nose turns pink when he
drinks. His wife, a well-born woman with the handwriting of
a small, slow-witted child.

DARIUS WHEELER
You are unreasonable and unkind.

SETSUKO HEARN
Am I? And why is it you may have as many lovers as you wish?
Why am I wrong that I would wish to enjoy the same? Fool-
ish to even ask. I wish I had been born a man.

CLAIRE TSONG
But you are not a man. I think sometimes that you forget.

SETSUKO HEARN
I do not forget.

(The sound of the shakuhachi flute changes tone. OWEN MATTHAISSEN,
ELIZABETH NEWMAN-ORR, *and* CLAIRE TSONG *recede from view.* SETSUKO
HEARN, DARIUS WHEELER, *and* JOHN BELL *remain.)*

JOHN BELL
This morning I hear the servants smashing snails with wooden
cudgels. There is something very satisfying in the sound.

SETSUKO HEARN

An inauspicious wind. My mood grows worse with each passing day. I am a terrible person, I think.

JOHN BELL

The sound of footsteps on nightingale floors
The echo of the temple bell
All the words I have not spoken—

(JOHN BELL *recedes from view.*)

SETSUKO HEARN

One night passes. And then a second, and then a third.
No word from Lord S. Another night and not a word.
How like an autumn leaf my passion, brittle and unlovely in its passing.

DARIUS WHEELER

A list of unsuitable things:

SETSUKO HEARN

A new lover who is no longer new.

DARIUS WHEELER

Hasty action followed by regret.

(*The sound of the shakuhachi flute changes tone.* DARIUS WHEELER *recedes from view.* JOHN BELL *appears at his desk.*)

SETSUKO HEARN

We pass each other in the garden.
The blossoms have long been swept away.
The taste of your lips, now bitter as unripe plums.

You are my one heart's truth. Did I ever tell you this? Did I ever speak this out loud? Would you have ever guessed?

(*The sound of the shakuhachi flute changes tone.* SETSUKO HEARN *transforms from Heian era lady to contemporary Western woman.*)

SETSUKO HEARN

It was summer when I went to sleep last night, yet when I awoke this morning, it was all of a sudden fall. The smell of foxfires at daybreak, ice drops on the branches of the trees. In the hills near Higashiyama, I heard a deer cry. I looked for you by the lake. There was a thick mist, I remember I could not see, and when I emerged from it at last, the leaves had all turned crimson in the night. Strange. Nothing is how it used to be.

*(The screen returns to its original image. A painting of a garden in au-
tumn: bare branches shrouded in mist. The sound of wooden clappers. The
screen vanishes. The sound of the shakuhachi flute ends.)*

Scene 18

(Light shift. Late afternoon of the same day. A corridor in the university.
SETSUKO HEARN *is looking through the transcript of the pillow book.*
DARIUS WHEELER *looks on.)*

SETSUKO HEARN
Where did you get this?

DARIUS WHEELER
It was found in a private library. It was sent to us for appraisal
by the owner. People send us stuff. Most of the time, it's not
worth the cost of shipping, but every so often, something
comes your way. You never know.

SETSUKO HEARN
Who did the translation?

DARIUS WHEELER
My assistant.

SETSUKO HEARN
Working from the original?

DARIUS WHEELER
From photos. This whole thing, to be honest, is kinda out of
my ken. My assistant gave me some background, smart guy,
but he's a little naive in some ways. I thought I'd run it by you,
see what you think.

SETSUKO HEARN
I don't know how to say this.

DARIUS WHEELER
Worthless, huh? You know, I gotta say I'm not surprised. I had
a feeling. I thought I'd bring it by, what the hell. Look, to tell
you the truth, what I really—

SETSUKO HEARN

No, wait. I don't think you understand.

(*The sound of wooden clappers.*)

SETSUKO HEARN

There's a quality, something in the voice, in the writing, it's uncanny. The batsubun, the epilogue, the interpolation of standard seasonal metaphors of transformation and loss, something in the syntax, the diction, even in translation—Utamakura, literally poem pillow, or pillow book. Heian era, eleventh century. The number of extant examples in the genre is practically nil. I don't know how I can articulate this to you. For something like this to turn up in this way, it would change everything, everything we thought we knew, all the assumptions we've made—well, it would, it would be premature to speculate. I'd love to get my hands on the original, if I could. If I could just, if I could examine the original. In the meantime, if I could take a look at those photos. The sooner the better.

DARIUS WHEELER

I'll get right on it.

SETSUKO HEARN

Forgive me.

DARIUS WHEELER

No, it would be my pleasure. I mean that.

SETSUKO HEARN

Thank you.

DARIUS WHEELER

So what are you doing now?

SETSUKO HEARN

I was just, I was going to go back to my office, do a little bit of work.

DARIUS WHEELER

Are you free for dinner? I know this place. It's not far. Just a few blocks away from here. Nothing fancy. How does that sound?

SETSUKO HEARN

That sounds—nice. Listen, why don't you meet me out front. I need to stop by my office on the way out, make a quick call. I'll just be a minute.

(*The sound of a tape rewinding.*)

Scene 19

(Light on ELIZABETH NEWMAN-ORR *removing hidden recording equipment taped to her skin. A fragment from a previous scene.)*

ELIZABETH NEWMAN-ORR
So what was the story? Who was she?

The sound of a tape rewinding.)

DARIUS WHEELER
Hardly any at all.

(The sound of wooden clappers.)

DARIUS WHEELER
Interested?

ELIZABETH NEWMAN-ORR
Another time perhaps.

DARIUS WHEELER
By then it'll be gone.

(The sound of a tape rewinding.)

ELIZABETH NEWMAN-ORR
I was given your name.

DARIUS WHEELER
Given my name by whom?

ELIZABETH NEWMAN-ORR
I'd rather not say.

(The sound of a tape rewinding.)

ELIZABETH NEWMAN-ORR
Can't we be candid with one another, Mr. Wheeler? I'd like that so much. It would make everything so much easier.

DARIUS WHEELER
What are we talking about?

ELIZABETH NEWMAN-ORR

I think you have an idea.

DARIUS WHEELER

Why don't you spell it out for me.

(*A phone begins to ring.* ELIZABETH NEWMAN-ORR *exits. Enter* JOHN BELL.)

Scene 20

(JOHN BELL *answers the phone in* WHEELER's *loft. Light on* OWEN MATTHIASSEN.)

JOHN BELL

Hello?

OWEN MATTHIASSEN

John, it's Owen Matthiassen. Is Darius there, by any chance?

JOHN BELL

No, Dr. Matthiassen, I'm afraid he's left for the day.

OWEN MATTHIASSEN

I see. Well, John, maybe you can help me. I was on the phone just now with my colleague Dr. Hearn, and she mentioned the most fascinating thing. A manuscript that turned up. Japanese. Heian era. Apparently, Darius brought the translation around for her to take a look at. I'm curious how he got a hold of the thing, where it came from, how it came to light. Do you know anything about this? You understand it could be immensely valuable, priceless even. Although I suppose everything eventually has a price.

(*The sound of wooden clappers. A dial tone.*)

OWEN MATTHIASSEN

Hello? John, are you still there? John—? John—?

(*The sound of a dial tone transforms into the sound of the shakuhachi flute. Light on the shoji panel where* JOHN BELL *previously drew the Japanese word. The sound of the flute grows, a single note sustained.* JOHN BELL *smashes his fist through the shoji panel, splitting the word apart. The sound of wooden clappers.*)

ACT TWO

Scene 21

(*Darkness. Scattered pages of paper are suspended in the darkness. The paper is distressed, ancient-seeming. The pages are dyed vermilion, rose, dayflower blue. Some are covered with a sprinkling of gold leaf and tiny Japanese lettering, kana. Light on* CLAIRE TSONG. *She examines a page, takes a lighter out of her pocket, sets the page on fire, lets it burn, then blows it out. She retrieves a Polaroid camera. She takes a picture of the page. A flash. Darkness.*)

Scene 22

(*A university lecture hall.* OWEN MATTHIASSEN *and* SETSUKO HEARN *are backstage. The ambient sound of voices in the audience.*)

OWEN MATTHIASSEN

I spoke with the dean this morning. Needless to say, he's taken a personal interest in the matter. I have to say I've never seen anything like it. I've been getting calls from all over the States, Europe, Japan. The media interest is overwhelming. When is Darius getting a hold of the original?

SETSUKO HEARN

In the next day or so.

OWEN MATTHIASSEN

Good, good. I have to confess, this whole thing, I'm afraid it's a little beyond my scope of expertise. I'm more of a general-

ist, as you know. I guess that's what they call us now—rather
euphemistically, I suspect. We're a dying breed. We used to
call ourselves Orientalists, and we studied the Orient. That's
how old I am. It was a different time, I suppose, a different
way of doing things. It's exciting, this whole thing, it's all very
exciting, and you should be, well, you should be pleased. So
then I'll say a few words, and then you can give them a little
bit of background, and then we'll take questions. Ready?

SETSUKO HEARN

Yes.

OWEN MATTHIASSEN

All right then—

(OWEN MATTHIASSEN *goes on stage. The sound of the audience grows
louder.* SETSUKO HEARN *remains backstage.*)

Scene 23

(*Light shift. Backstage of a press conference.* OWEN MATTHIASSEN
is speaking into a microphone. He is a distant figure. SETSUKO HEARN
remains in the foreground.)

OWEN MATTHIASSEN

Ladies—gentlemen—please—if I could have your attention—
I cannot stress enough the significance of this manuscript.
Even in its fragmentary state, its impact on our field of schol-
arship is immeasurable—

(OWEN MATTHIASSEN *continues to speak. His words grow faint. The sound
of wooden clappers. Silence.*)

Scene 24

(A park near the university. Autumn. Crimson leaves, bare branches against the sky. SETSUKO HEARN *and* DARIUS WHEELER *are looking at Polaroids of the original manuscript. The middle of a conversation.)*

DARIUS WHEELER

There's some damage. You can see it, here and here. It's not the end of the world, but the sooner we can get a hold of it, get it in a climatized setting, the better.

SETSUKO HEARN

When do you think that will be?

DARIUS WHEELER

Tomorrow or the day after. Trust me. This part I know.

SETSUKO HEARN

Over a thousand years old—it's like a dream. You dream about this sort of thing, that lightning will strike, and maybe you'll be lucky enough to be there when it does. At least I do. I mean, I have. I guess everybody has at some point or another. Did you know—

DARIUS WHEELER

Tell me.

SETSUKO HEARN

Did you know that men of Heian era Japan wrote in Chinese, a language not their own, and one in which most gained only, at best, a schoolboy proficiency—

DARIUS WHEELER

Is that right—

SETSUKO HEARN

But Heian era women, by contrast, wrote almost exclusively in their native tongue, allowing them, I think, a kind of emotional clarity, an immediacy, a seamless correspondence between the inchoate thought and the written word. One might even go so far as to say that because they wrote in their native tongue, they were able to write with a candor and transparency virtually impossible for their male contemporaries.

DARIUS WHEELER

Now that seems very, very doctrinaire.

SETSUKO HEARN

Perhaps. Let's say instead that they wrote without artifice. They wrote about their innermost feelings—feelings of restlessness, uncertainty, desire, doubt. Modern, almost modern in their insights, oddly familiar, they wrote in a voice that was singular and unmistakably female—

(*The sound of wooden clappers.*)

SETSUKO HEARN

How is your hand?

(DARIUS WHEELER *holds out his hand.*)

SETSUKO HEARN

I can barely see where it was. What? What is it?

DARIUS WHEELER

Nothing. It's just you're so beautiful.

SETSUKO HEARN

I wonder how many women you've said that to. I'm guessing quite a few.

DARIUS WHEELER

What if I told you this was different?

SETSUKO HEARN

I don't think I'd believe you.

DARIUS WHEELER

You've got to be the most beautiful skeptic I've ever met.

SETSUKO HEARN

I'm afraid flattery needs to be a little more subtle than that.

DARIUS WHEELER

I know, I know how I sound. I know what you're thinking, and you know what, normally you'd be right.

SETSUKO HEARN

But not now.

DARIUS WHEELER

No, not now. You don't believe me.

SETSUKO HEARN

What I believe is that there are words—

DARIUS WHEELER

Yes—

SETSUKO HEARN

And then there are the feelings and thoughts behind the words, and that the relationship between the two is neither reliable nor precise, nor is it maybe meant to be—

DARIUS WHEELER

No—?

SETSUKO HEARN

No, and that maybe the space between what we say and what we do, what we see and what we feel, that it's necessary, the space where anything can happen. Chaos, confusion, terrible, terrible confusion—

(DARIUS WHEELER *and* SETSUKO HEARN *kiss.*)

SETSUKO HEARN

OK, you know what, this is really, this is not a good idea. I don't know you, and you don't know me, and whatever this is, it's based on nothing, a first impression.

DARIUS WHEELER

Love at first sight.

SETSUKO HEARN

Please.

DARIUS WHEELER

You don't believe in that.

SETSUKO HEARN

No. No, I don't.

DARIUS WHEELER

It's kinda old-fashioned.

SETSUKO HEARN

It's also very convenient.

DARIUS WHEELER

Look all I want—what I want—is for you to entertain, just for
a second, the possibility that maybe what I'm saying to you,
what I'm trying to say to you, that it's—

SETSUKO HEARN

What? The truth?

DARIUS WHEELER

Yes.

SETSUKO HEARN

Ah I see. What if we were truthful? What if we were good?
What if desire were the same as love? What if it were all simple and clear?

DARIUS WHEELER

Maybe it is. Maybe sometimes it is.

SETSUKO HEARN

You know, I don't think so.

DARIUS WHEELER

How can you know that. How can you know for sure?

SETSUKO HEARN

Because nothing is that easy. In the world I live in, nothing is
ever that easy.

(*The sound of wooden clappers.*)

DARIUS WHEELER

I like you so much.

(*The sound of wooden clappers.*)

DARIUS WHEELER

Everything I say sounds like a line. I know that. I know that.
I'm blowing it, aren't I?

SETSUKO HEARN

It depends on what you're trying to do.

DARIUS WHEELER

Make you like me just a little. Something like that.

SETSUKO HEARN
I like you.

(*The sound of wooden clappers.*)

SETSUKO HEARN
It's that I look at you and I don't know what I'm seeing. What
am I seeing?

DARIUS WHEELER
A deeply fucked-up individual.

SETSUKO HEARN
Is that right?

DARIUS WHEELER
The worst. And the funny thing is—this is the funny thing—
he's fallen for this woman who happens to see through all his
bullshit, this beautiful, brilliant woman, and he can barely talk
when he's around her, which I know is kinda hard to believe,
but it's true, and I know, I know right now he sounds like an
idiot and a jerk, probably because he is an idiot and a jerk, and
she should probably tell him to just get lost, but I really—I
hope she doesn't, I really hope she doesn't.

(DARIUS WHEELER *and* SETSUKO HEARN *are very close. The sound of a
phone ringing.*)

Scene 25

(CLAIRE TSONG'S *work space.* JOHN BELL *is studying the pages from the
top of the act. They're pages from the "original" manuscript, distressed
paper, ancient-seeming, with Japanese lettering, colored paper sprinkled
with gold leaf.* CLAIRE TSONG *is changing out of paint-spattered work
clothes into dress clothes. She puts on make-up, fixes her hair, transform-
ing herself. The phone continues to ring.*)

CLAIRE TSONG
Mulberry paper. Carbon-based ink. A little dirt, a little fire, a
little tea—are you going to get that or what?

(*The phone stops ringing.*)

JOHN BELL

The calligraphy—

CLAIRE TSONG

Authentic. I know.

JOHN BELL

How did you do this?

CLAIRE TSONG

Honey, I'm just the midwife to your genius. Analyze the brushstroke. Hold it up to the light. I'm a very gifted girl. If you didn't know better, if you saw this under Plexiglas in some museum somewhere—

JOHN BELL

But it's not real.

CLAIRE TSONG

Isn't it? It looks pretty real to me.

JOHN BELL

It's not about what it looks like. It's about what it is. Eventually somebody's going to figure out the difference.

CLAIRE TSONG

And what if they don't?

(*The sound of wooden clappers.*)

CLAIRE TSONG

Provenance.

JOHN BELL

Claire—

CLAIRE TSONG

All you need to do is piece together a credible paper trail: a bill of sale, a catalogue reference, cut and paste, some signatures—

JOHN BELL

It's not that easy. Do you have any idea how many calls we've been getting? Everybody wants to see the original.

CLAIRE TSONG

Good thing we have it.

JOHN BELL

No, Claire, no. We have no original because there is no original, because even the so-called "original" is not an original.

CLAIRE TSONG

I guess it all depends on how you define "original."

JOHN BELL

You know, I define it the way I think most everybody else does. It's the thing that's real as opposed to the thing that's fake. I think it's pretty clearcut. Jesus Christ, what am I doing, what the hell am I doing? I feel like an impostor.

CLAIRE TSONG

That's because you are.

JOHN BELL

No, see, Claire, you're wrong. I'm not. This was not my idea. This was never my idea.

CLAIRE TSONG

No?

JOHN BELL

I didn't want this.

CLAIRE TSONG

You didn't want what? You didn't want to write what you wrote? You didn't want to get paid for doing what you do? You didn't want to take credit for something you did for once in your life? Can you maybe own up, John, can you maybe try?

JOHN BELL

We're different, OK, we see things differently. I'm not like you.

CLAIRE TSONG

You know, I think you are. I think you're exactly like me. I just don't think you realize it yet.

(*The sound of wooden clappers.*)

CLAIRE TSONG

Look, just think of it as a little insurance policy. Somebody sniffs it out, you say you were duped, no harm, no foul.

JOHN BELL

I wish he'd never seen it. I don't know why I left it out in the first place. It was so stupid. I should've seen this coming, I should've known. What was I thinking?

CLAIRE TSONG

What were you thinking?

(*The sound of wooden clappers.*)

CLAIRE TSONG

All right, lookit, Wheeler needs to buy before he can sell. In order to sell the manuscript—the "original," that is—he needs to own it, and he doesn't own it.

JOHN BELL

Not yet. He wants me to talk to the guy, a guy who doesn't exist, get him to sell a thing, a thing that doesn't exist. This is insane, this whole thing is insane.

CLAIRE TSONG

Do it. If Wheeler wants to buy it, let him. You pick the price. Just remember, make it steep. The higher the price, the more desirable. We can split it, fifty-fifty.

JOHN BELL

I don't believe you, Claire. What kind of person thinks like this? It's like you planned this whole thing from the start.

CLAIRE TSONG

Doll, I couldn't have planned this if I wanted to. I just seized the day is all.

JOHN BELL

What about Wheeler?

CLAIRE TSONG

What about him?

JOHN BELL

I don't know, Claire—call me a nut, but I think he's maybe going to sue us, and then I think he's maybe going to have criminal charges brought against us, and then I think we're maybe going to go to jail.

CLAIRE TSONG

That's not going to happen.

JOHN BELL

How can you be so sure?

(The sound of wooden clappers.)

CLAIRE TSONG

Because I know him. I know his mind, I know how it works.
I know him. He'd rather save face and eat the loss. Trust me.
He's not going to say a word.

(The sound of wooden clappers. Bukkaeri, a Kabuki costume-change in which the upper half of the costume falls down over the lower half revealing a new pattern. CLAIRE TSONG's *appearance has completely transformed.)*

JOHN BELL

Claire—

CLAIRE TSONG

Look, just talk to him, set it up, call me when you're done.
(Picking up the pages of the "original" manuscript) Here, we don't want these lying around here, do we— What?

JOHN BELL

I don't know. Nothing. You just, I don't know, you look different.

CLAIRE TSONG

I just changed my clothes. That's all.

*(*CLAIRE TSONG *exits. A version of the Kitsune Roppo exit, a kind of Kabuki exit marked by leaps and bounds.* JOHN BELL *vanishes. The sound of the shakuhachi flute begins.)*

Scene 26

(A shunga. An erotic woodblock print. The sound of the shakuhachi flute continues. Light shift. Two lovers in the shadows. Glimpses of naked flesh. The sound of breathing. A disembodied voice, faint and faraway, a recorded echo of what came before.)

SETSUKO HEARN

No rain tonight, no moon, the air is perfectly still
Not even the faintest breeze stirs the leaves.

In the pool in the garden below, carp swim beneath the surface—
Flashes of white in the murky green
Their bellies slick and wet—
The tickle of waterweed
The soft wet moss—
The curve of your neck, your fingertips
The rustle of silk undone—
Your mouth, your tongue
Your lips, the taste of your lips, salt, wet
The warmth of your breath against my skin—

Scene 27

(The sound of the shakuhachi flute continues. Light on OWEN MATTHIASSEN. *Visible behind him is the fake Hokusai print of Mount Fuji.)*

OWEN MATTHIASSEN

Footnote number twenty-seven: *Ibid, opus cit.* Prevalent throughout the text is a sensibility the Japanese call *mono no aware*, i.e., an awareness of imminent loss, a melancholic perspective one finds throughout the history of Japanese literature. Loosely translated, *mono no aware* is the phenomenon by which one perceives the beauty of a thing only in the moment of recognizing its essential impermanence. Seasons pass. Flowers wither and die. Indeed, it is precisely this delimited life span which lends an object its beauty, which endows it with value, and renders it precious—no, not precious, not precious—priceless— priceless in our eyes.

(The sound of wooden clappers. OWEN MATTHIASSEN *and the fake print recede from view.)*

Scene 28

(*Light on* SETSUKO HEARN *and* DARIUS WHEELER. *They dress.*)

DARIUS WHEELER

What was she like?

SETSUKO HEARN

We don't really know. The details of her life, the circumstances that brought her to court, her name even are all unknown. Which is often the case.

DARIUS WHEELER

I have this image of her in my mind.

SETSUKO HEARN

Do you? Well, we know—what do we know—we know her skin was very white, and that she whitened it further with a cream made from nightingale droppings. We know she plucked the entirety of her eyebrows, and blackened her teeth, as was the fashion of the day, and that she wore multiple layers of kimono—colorful, complicated, coded in a language of symbols, hidden meanings, of which we have only inklings. The Heian-era court in which she lived was a highly literate, highly aestheticized society. Like her peers, she spent her days writing poetry and preparing for the many festivals that marked the passing of the seasons. We know she was unmarried and during her time at court, she engaged in multiple romantic liaisons with both men and women. This alone is a remarkable revelation. As an articulation of transgressive sexuality and a revisioning of gender stereotypes prevalent in a patriarchal culture—you know, I'm talking an awful lot.

DARIUS WHEELER

You have a lot to say.

SETSUKO HEARN

Yes. Yes, I do.

DARIUS WHEELER
What do you think happened to her? Afterwards, I mean.

SETSUKO HEARN
Maybe she left the court and married a provincial lord. Maybe she lived her final years as a Buddhist nun, chanting sutras in a temple. The fragment ends abruptly. We won't ever know with any degree of certainty. We can only speculate.

DARIUS WHEELER
Do you think she was happy?

SETSUKO HEARN
I don't know. I'm not sure. Perhaps. I mean I'm not sure I know what happy means.

DARIUS WHEELER
Happy means happy.

SETSUKO HEARN
Happy means happy, beautiful means beautiful. Oh to live in the world you live in. What a great world. Everything's so clearcut, so simple.

DARIUS WHEELER
Sometimes things just are what they are, they mean what they mean.

SETSUKO HEARN
So I've heard. What? What is it?

DARIUS WHEELER
I want very much, I want to make you happy.

(*The sound of wooden clappers.*)

SETSUKO HEARN
I need to go. I need to get back to work.

DARIUS WHEELER
What if I say, I don't want you to.

SETSUKO HEARN
Then I would say, "But I have to."

DARIUS WHEELER
And I would say, "But I won't let you."

SETSUKO HEARN

Would you really say that?

DARIUS WHEELER

I might.

SETSUKO HEARN

Then I would say, "Unhand me, sir."

DARIUS WHEELER

"Unhand me?"

SETSUKO HEARN

Yes.

DARIUS WHEELER

I like that. It's quaint.

SETSUKO HEARN

I'm quaint.

DARIUS WHEELER

Are you quaint?

SETSUKO HEARN

Very, very quaint. You'd be surprised.

(SETSUKO HEARN *and* DARIUS WHEELER *kiss.*)

SETSUKO HEARN

I have to get back to the office. I've got a stack of work waiting for me and about a million calls to return, and I need to proof the draft of the article, I'm almost done—

DARIUS WHEELER

Dinner later? What about drinks? How about dinner and drinks, how about a nightcap—

SETSUKO HEARN

I don't know—

DARIUS WHEELER

Say yes.

SETSUKO HEARN

I don't know, I don't know—

DARIUS WHEELER

I won't let you go until you say yes. Say yes, please say yes.

SETSUKO HEARN

Yes.

(*The sound of wooden clappers.* SETSUKO HEARN *exits.* DARIUS WHEELER *remains. Enter* ELIZABETH NEWMAN-ORR.)

Scene 29

(*The hanging scroll from the top of the play appears. Portrait of a lady, Kamakura era, gilt background.* WHEELER'S *loft space, later that day.*)

ELIZABETH NEWMAN-ORR

Mr. Wheeler, you seem distracted.

DARIUS WHEELER

I'm sorry, what were you saying?

ELIZABETH NEWMAN-ORR

Just that I was running a little late. I called, but there was no answer. I got here as fast as I could. I take it there were no problems.

DARIUS WHEELER

No. None.

(*Enter* JOHN BELL *pushing a dolley on which rests a large box. He parks the dolley, and begins prying the front lid of the box open with a crowbar. It's a noisy and violent opening up.*)

DARIUS WHEELER

Everything went smoothly. It arrived early this morning.

ELIZABETH NEWMAN-ORR

I'm impressed. So efficient. I have to hand it to you. You have a knack, but I wonder if you ever have any qualms.

DARIUS WHEELER

Qualms about what?

ELIZABETH NEWMAN-ORR

Breaking the law.

DARIUS WHEELER

I don't think about it that way.

ELIZABETH NEWMAN-ORR

How do you think about it?

DARIUS WHEELER

I don't, Ms. Orr. I think your question is a philosophical one, and I'm not much of a philosopher, I'm afraid.

ELIZABETH NEWMAN-ORR

It's such an interesting business, the business you're in. It's fascinating. You know, I read an item in the paper just this morning. About an ancient manuscript that was sent to you for appraisal. I understand it could be quite valuable.

DARIUS WHEELER

Yes.

ELIZABETH NEWMAN-ORR

But now you don't own it, do you—the original, that is?

DARIUS WHEELER

No.

ELIZABETH NEWMAN-ORR

You're just a representative.

DARIUS WHEELER

An interested party, yes.

ELIZABETH NEWMAN-ORR

I wonder how much that manuscript would fetch on the open market—the original, I mean?

DARIUS WHEELER

It's an interesting question.

ELIZABETH NEWMAN-ORR

I think so.

DARIUS WHEELER

You're full of interesting questions.

ELIZABETH NEWMAN-ORR

I try.

DARIUS WHEELER

I have a few interesting questions of my own.

ELIZABETH NEWMAN-ORR

Oh?

DARIUS WHEELER

For starters, I wonder who you are and why you're here. I have to say, I have an idea.

(JOHN BELL *pries the last nail loose. The front lid of the box crashes open. Revealed inside the box is a painting on silk. A portrait of a lady seemingly identical to the portrait of a lady already hanging in* DARIUS WHEELER'S *loft.*)

ELIZABETH NEWMAN-ORR

She has a twin.

DARIUS WHEELER

Not exactly.

ELIZABETH NEWMAN-ORR

I'm afraid I don't follow.

DARIUS WHEELER

This is a fake. I saw it once at a party at that villa on Lugard Road, had a chance to look at it up close. I didn't need to. I could tell it was a fake from a mile away. All you need to do is look at it a while. You'll see what I mean. I hope you like it, I really do, because you and whoever you work for just paid an awful lot of money for it. Is your mike picking me up—this is key— in order for this little exposé of yours to work—and I think that's what this was, I may be wrong, it's just a hunch— this painting needs to be authentic, an actual antiquity a country of origin would hate to see go. Because it's not, you have no crime, you barely have an impropriety, all you have is the purchase and transport of a second-rate fake for a large, some might say, absurdly large sum of money. But who am I to judge. In art, as in life, there's no accounting for taste. Your line producer didn't do his homework, Ms. Orr. In the future, you and he—forgive me, he or she—are going to have to do better than that.

(*The sound of wooden clappers.*)

ELIZABETH NEWMAN-ORR

If it's a crime to transport a national treasure, surely it's a crime to own one.

(*The sound of wooden clappers.*)

ELIZABETH NEWMAN-ORR

Oh. I see. Yours is a fake, too.

DARIUS WHEELER

You know, there are fakes, and then there are fakes. Some fakes are obvious, and some are pretty good. Some are so good, in fact, it's hard to be sure one way or another without carbon dating, auto-radiography, all kinds of tests you'd have to get my permission to run. She is after all my property, and last I checked, that still counted for something.

ELIZABETH NEWMAN-ORR

You're very pleased with yourself, aren't you?

DARIUS WHEELER

I'm actually wracked with self-loathing.

ELIZABETH NEWMAN-ORR

Somehow I find that hard to believe.

DARIUS WHEELER

I hide it well. I think you know the way out. If not—

ELIZABETH NEWMAN-ORR

That's quite all right. I think I can manage. Thank you for your time, Mr. Wheeler and Mr.—

JOHN BELL

Bell.

ELIZABETH NEWMAN-ORR

Mr. Bell. Good day, Mr. Wheeler. Mr. Bell.

(*The sound of wooden clappers.* ELIZABETH NEWMAN-ORR *exits.*)

Scene 30

(JOHN BELL *and* DARIUS WHEELER *study each other from a distance.*)

JOHN BELL

It's not a fake.

DARIUS WHEELER

No.

JOHN BELL

I didn't think so. I mean I didn't think it was.

DARIUS WHEELER

I lied, John. People lie. Sometimes they get caught, sometimes they don't. It depends on who they're lying to.

JOHN BELL

No, I understand, I understand completely.

DARIUS WHEELER

So?

JOHN BELL

Yeah?

DARIUS WHEELER

What's the story?

JOHN BELL

Sorry?

DARIUS WHEELER

The manuscript. How's it looking?

JOHN BELL

It's looking good, it's looking really good.

DARIUS WHEELER

Good.

JOHN BELL

He wants to sell.

DARIUS WHEELER

Great. What's he asking?

JOHN BELL

One million.

DARIUS WHEELER

Dollars.

JOHN BELL

Pounds. Pounds sterling.

(*The sound of wooden clappers.*)

JOHN BELL

But I get the sense, from the little bit I know, that it's just an arbitrary figure, a stab in the dark, because frankly I'm not really sure, you know, I'm not really sure he knows what he's doing.

DARIUS WHEELER

Tell him we'll have a courier ready with a check before the close of business. Or we can do a direct money transfer, Channel Islands account. It's his call. The thing I wonder is why he'd go so low. He could get twice that much, if he wanted to, more.

JOHN BELL

Maybe he doesn't realize what he has. You know, I don't know. I don't really know him.

DARIUS WHEELER

People are mysterious, aren't they, why they do what they do.

JOHN BELL

I guess so, yeah.

DARIUS WHEELER

Well, whatever it is, I want you to make the call right away, nail it down, last thing I want is cold feet and a bidding war. Oh and John—

(*The sound of wooden clappers.*)

DARIUS WHEELER

Don't think I'm not aware of everything you've done. I am. When this is all settled, I want us to sit down together and have a talk. I want to talk about your future.

(*The sound of wooden clappers. Exit* DARIUS WHEELER. JOHN BELL *picks up the phone and dials. He exits listening as the phone rings on the other end of the line.*)

Scene 31

(*Light shift.* DARIUS WHEELER'*s loft. An hour later. Enter* CLAIRE TSONG *in new clothes she changed into earlier. She has a package containing the original manuscript. She studies the two paintings, the two portraits of a lady, one real, one fake. Re-enter* ELIZABETH NEWMAN-ORR)

CLAIRE TSONG

Hey.

(*The sound of wooden clappers.*)

ELIZABETH NEWMAN-ORR

Hey.

CLAIRE TSONG

Looking for Wheeler?

ELIZABETH NEWMAN-ORR

No, I'm actually, I'm looking for Mr. Bell. Is he in, do you know?

CLAIRE TSONG

He should be. I was just looking for him myself.

ELIZABETH NEWMAN-ORR

I'd love to talk to him.

CLAIRE TSONG

He's a very interesting guy.

ELIZABETH NEWMAN-ORR

I sense that.

CLAIRE TSONG

He knows all kinds of things.

ELIZABETH NEWMAN-ORR

I sense that, too.

CLAIRE TSONG

More than he lets on.

ELIZABETH NEWMAN-ORR

Do I know you? I do, don't I? We met the other night, at the party for Utagawa. I didn't, I didn't recognize you. New outfit. And your hair, it's different.

CLAIRE TSONG

Yeah, it's—well, yeah it's different.

ELIZABETH NEWMAN-ORR

I like it.

CLAIRE TSONG

Yeah?

ELIZABETH NEWMAN-ORR

No, it's very, it's really, it's pretty.

CLAIRE TSONG

Thanks, thank you. Claire.

ELIZABETH NEWMAN-ORR

Beth.

CLAIRE TSONG

It's nice to see you again.

ELIZABETH NEWMAN-ORR

Yeah.

CLAIRE TSONG

Are you OK?

ELIZABETH NEWMAN-ORR

Yeah, no, I'm fine. It's just, it's been a really shitty day. You know how that goes. You're an artist. I remember. Mixed media.

CLAIRE TSONG

Very good. And you? What do you do? I don't think you ever said.

ELIZABETH NEWMAN-ORR

I'm a writer, a journalist actually. I was working on a piece. It didn't quite pan out the way I'd planned. I thought maybe Mr. Bell, I thought maybe he might—well, I don't know what I was thinking. How do you know Wheeler? You know—never mind. I don't even care anymore. He's a piece of work, that guy.

CLAIRE TSONG

He's a prick.

ELIZABETH NEWMAN-ORR

I'm so glad I'm not the only one who thinks so.

CLAIRE TSONG

You're not.

(The sound of wooden clappers.)

CLAIRE TSONG

So you're a journalist, huh?

ELIZABETH NEWMAN-ORR

Not a very good one and probably not for long—but yes, in theory, yes.

CLAIRE TSONG

Listen, you want to maybe, you want to go for a drink? You look like you could use a drink.

ELIZABETH NEWMAN-ORR
What about Mr. Bell?

CLAIRE TSONG
John? We'll catch up with him later. After you.

(CLAIRE TSONG *and* ELIZABETH NEWMAN-ORR *exit. The sound of wooden clappers.*)

Scene 32

(OWEN MATTHIASSEN *and* SETSUKO HEARN *in* OWEN MATTHIASSEN*'s office. The fake Hokusai print hangs on the wall.* OWEN MATTHIASSEN *is holding a xeroxed copy of the transcript.*)

OWEN MATTHIASSEN
Have you ever seen Mount Fuji? In real life, I mean?

SETSUKO HEARN
Once. Through the window of a passing train.

OWEN MATTHIASSEN
You were lucky. Half the time it's covered in clouds, you can't see a thing. Hokusai was an old man when he made his study of the mountain. He came up with forty-six views; why they call the series thirty-six views—well, things are sometimes more than they seem to be, I suppose. Or less. If he'd lived longer, I suspect there would've been more. The permutations are infinite. How we look at the thing itself, which part we're able to see, if we're able to see it at all.

(*The sound of wooden clappers.*)

SETSUKO HEARN
Dr. Matthiassen—

OWEN MATTHIASSEN
(*Paging through the xeroxed copy*)
In fairness, it wouldn't have even occurred to me, if I hadn't gotten the call from that journalist—I've forgotten her name. She's apparently seen the actual forgery, interviewed the forger.

The story will air sometime next week. The text was very convincing, I must say. And of course, the photos were a nice touch. The thing is, though, and this is the awkward thing, it was all right here in front of us the whole time. Anomalies, inconsistencies. "On the fifteenth day of the eighth month, we catch fireflies . . . A visiting sage entertains us with his parrot." The parrot—non-indigenous, virtually unheard of in Heian era Japan. "I received your letter in the morning on violet paper bound with plumeria." Plumeria. Again another non-indigenous species, anomalous, completely anomalous. The list goes on. At first I ascribed it to flaws in transcription, a certain license taken in translation, but the sheer volume of discrepancies, it's overwhelming. When I look at the text now, all I see are anomalies. Once you begin to look, you see, it gives itself away.

(*The sound of wooden clappers.* OWEN MATTHIASSEN *fades away.* SETSUKO HEARN *remains in the foreground.*)

Scene 33

(*Light shift.* WHEELER's *loft. Early evening of the same day.* SETSUKO HEARN *is looking at two virtually identical paintings of the lady, one original, the other fake.* DARIUS WHEELER *is preparing drinks. He gives one to* SETSUKO HEARN. *The middle of a conversation.*)

SETSUKO HEARN
Tell me something about yourself.

DARIUS WHEELER
What do you want to know?

SETSUKO HEARN
I don't know where to begin. Where do I begin?

DARIUS WHEELER
Who was your first true love?

SETSUKO HEARN
Who was your first true love?

DARIUS WHEELER

Suzanne Henig. I was fifteen. She broke my heart.

SETSUKO HEARN

You've had other loves since.

DARIUS WHEELER

One.

SETSUKO HEARN

Only one?

DARIUS WHEELER

I've had affections.

SETSUKO HEARN

Which is different?

DARIUS WHEELER

Which is different, yes.

SETSUKO HEARN

Were you ever married?

DARIUS WHEELER

No. And you?

SETSUKO HEARN

Once. A long time ago. It lasted less than a year. I think we were friends more than we were lovers. We're still friends. We talk on the phone every so often. He's married, a father. I think we wanted different things.

DARIUS WHEELER

What did you want?

SETSUKO HEARN

To be very good at what I do.

DARIUS WHEELER

Ambitious.

SETSUKO HEARN

I used to be embarrassed by that word, but then I stopped. It's pointless to pretend to be something you're not. We make certain choices, some without even realizing. Tell me something else. Where are you from? Where did you grow up?

DARIUS WHEELER

Bellingham, Washington.

SETSUKO HEARN

Iowa. Fairfield, Iowa.

DARIUS WHEELER

That's not what I would've guessed.

SETSUKO HEARN

What would you have guessed?

DARIUS WHEELER

Tokyo. Los Angeles. I don't know.

SETSUKO HEARN

My father was a missionary in Japan. When he came back, he wanted to go home. Iowa was home. Did you have brothers and sisters?

DARIUS WHEELER

A sister. She lives on Mercer Island. On a clear day, you can see Mount Rainier. It's like a picture. It's, it's beautiful. And you?

SETSUKO HEARN

Only child.

DARIUS WHEELER

Your mother was Japanese.

SETSUKO HEARN

I was adopted actually. From an orphanage in Hangzhou. I was there until I was almost two. I'm Chinese by birth. My mother, my adopted mother, her family is Japanese.

DARIUS WHEELER

And your father?

SETSUKO HEARN

Scotch-Irish, a little German, you know, mixed. When I was growing up, people saw me, and they just assumed I was my parents' daughter—which of course, in almost every way, I am.

DARIUS WHEELER

Do you remember China?

SETSUKO HEARN

No. If no one had told me, I would never have known, I would never have even guessed. My earliest memories are of corn-fields and big sky and college football. My dad was a big college football fan.

DARIUS WHEELER

Hawkeyes?

SETSUKO HEARN

You bet. Huge. Help me.

DARIUS WHEELER

What were you like as a little girl?

SETSUKO HEARN

Very studious. Very idealistic. I wanted to find out things, all kinds of things. And I believed I could. I think I was, in retrospect, very sheltered.

DARIUS WHEELER

Were you happy?

SETSUKO HEARN

Yes. Yes, I was.

DARIUS WHEELER

Listen—

SETSUKO HEARN

—No, please. Tell me something, tell me something else.

DARIUS WHEELER

I don't know what to say. What can I say?

SETSUKO HEARN

Who do you look like, your mother or your father?

DARIUS WHEELER

My father.

SETSUKO HEARN

And are you like him?

DARIUS WHEELER

In a way, I guess. He was an amateur collector. Collected woodblock prints. Got hooked when he was in the navy, stationed in Tokyo right after the war. He'd keep his prints between sheets of transparent paper. It gave him great pleasure. When I was eight, he took us back to Japan. He bought this Hokusai print on that trip, found it in a little hole in the wall in Shinagawa. Mount Fuji at sunset, crimson sky, seen across the Bay of Kuroda. He paid a lot of money for it, more than he had to spend. Ten years later, I remember coming home, and looking at it and realizing it was a fake.

SETSUKO HEARN

Did you tell him?

DARIUS WHEELER

No.

SETSUKO HEARN

But you thought less of him.

DARIUS WHEELER

My father loved the print. He loved it with a big and undiscerning heart. It didn't matter if it wasn't what he thought it was.

SETSUKO HEARN

Love is blind. Is that the moral of the story?

DARIUS WHEELER

Listen to me—

SETSUKO HEARN

I should've known better. I should've seen this for what it was. Don't.

(*The sound of wooden clappers.*)

SETSUKO HEARN

I tendered my resignation today, I take full responsibility for this, I'm the one to blame, it was my mistake. The only question I'm left with is what you stood to gain. What did you stand to gain? Money, I suppose—

DARIUS WHEELER

You think I knew. You think I'd do that to you —

SETSUKO HEARN

I suppose you needed somebody to certify the authenticity of your property, to ensure its value prior to sale—

DARIUS WHEELER

That's not what this is about—

SETSUKO HEARN

What is this about? Why don't you tell me what this is all about.

DARIUS WHEELER

It's not what you think—

SETSUKO HEARN

What I think? How dare you. What do I think? Tell me, what do I think?

DARIUS WHEELER

That I somehow, that I used you. Listen to me—

SETSUKO HEARN

I was so stupid, I can't believe how stupid I was—

DARIUS WHEELER

You made a mistake—

SETSUKO HEARN

My mistake was having anything to do with someone like you—

DARIUS WHEELER

All right, look, don't pretend to be some kind of innocent—

SETSUKO HEARN

What are you saying—

DARIUS WHEELER

You think you are above reproach, you think you're pure, that you're some kind of victim—

SETSUKO HEARN

What are you saying—

DARIUS WHEELER

You were the one who wanted this. I just picked up the tab, and you were happy to let me—

SETSUKO HEARN

You disgust me, everything about you disgusts me—

DARIUS WHEELER

I did this for you. This was all for you. Listen to me—

SETSUKO HEARN

Don't.

(SETSUKO HEARN *drops her glass. It shatters. The clear liquid pools on the floor. In the light, it looks red.*)

SETSUKO HEARN

You actually seemed, for a moment, you seemed sincere. I believed you. I wanted to believe you.

(*The sound of wooden clappers.* SETSUKO HEARN *exits.* DARIUS WHEELER *disappears from view.*)

Scene 34

(*A gallery. 36 paintings are revealed hanging in the space. From a distance, each painting looks like a canvas filled with flecks of color.* CLAIRE TSONG *is cleaning up a broken glass. She sweeps up the pieces. Enter* ELIZABETH NEWMAN-ORR *with two drinks.*)

CLAIRE TSONG

It slipped.

ELIZABETH NEWMAN-ORR

I got you another. Excited?

CLAIRE TSONG

Nervous.

ELIZABETH NEWMAN-ORR

Don't be. Everything looks perfect. (*Giving* CLAIRE TSONG *her drink*)

(ELIZABETH NEWMAN-ORR *and* CLAIRE TSONG *drink. The sound of wooden clappers.*)

CLAIRE TSONG

So? How did the interview with Wheeler go? What did he say?

ELIZABETH NEWMAN-ORR

Lots of things. He claims he didn't know. He claims he didn't know a thing. He says he was fooled like everyone else.

CLAIRE TSONG

Don't tell me you believe him.

ELIZABETH NEWMAN-ORR

You know, I kinda do. When we were editing the tape, he seemed—I don't know—I hate to say it, but he seemed kinda truthful.

CLAIRE TSONG

Did he?

(*The sound of wooden clappers.*)

CLAIRE TSONG

When you were interviewing him, did he ever tell you about how he got started, in his business, I mean?

ELIZABETH NEWMAN-ORR

I don't know, he told me a story, he told me some story about his father.

CLAIRE TSONG

That's not the story I'm talking about. It takes money, you know. You need a little nut, some capital to start a business like Wheeler had. He met this girl—he didn't tell you about the girl? Maybe it slipped his mind. This was a while ago. She was very young. She had some stuff, some artwork she'd inherited when her parents died, some scrolls, a screen, what turned out to be a celadon vase. She knew he knew a thing or two about Asian art. She asked him what he thought. He said it was all pretty much worthless, but he'd buy it all from her, if she wanted, for a lump sum, a very modest sum. She was an art student at the time. There were debts. She needed the cash. A year later, she sees this painting that used to belong to her parents. It's in a Christies catalogue, along with some other stuff he bought from her. The whole lot ended up selling for just under two million. She saw him later at a party in Boston. He said that art and business were two different things. That he hoped she was better at art than she was at business. And that he'd give her a job, if she wanted, doing restoration. She could make good money.

ELIZABETH NEWMAN-ORR

And she threw her drink in his face.

(*The sound of wooden clappers.*)

CLAIRE TSONG

She may have.

ELIZABETH NEWMAN-ORR

She sounds like an unusual girl.

CLAIRE TSONG

I don't know. I think, at the end of the day, she's just your run-of-the-mill, girl-next-door kinda girl.

ELIZABETH NEWMAN-ORR

I don't know about that.

CLAIRE TSONG

I guess she's a lot of things. I guess she's kinda complicated.

ELIZABETH NEWMAN-ORR

I like complicated.

CLAIRE TSONG

Yeah? I'm glad.

(CLAIRE TSONG *and* ELIZABETH NEWMAN-ORR *kiss. The sound of wooden clappers. They disappear from view.*)

Scene 35

(*A gallery. The 36 paintings remain. The ambient sound of voices, laughter from another room in the gallery. Enter* JOHN BELL *in new clothes. Enter* OWEN MATTHIASSEN.)

OWEN MATTHIASSEN

John.

JOHN BELL

Dr. Matthiassen. How are you?

OWEN MATTHIASSEN

Well, I'm doing well. I didn't know you were a fan of Utagawa's work.

JOHN BELL

My friend—well, she, she helped put this all together.

OWEN MATTHIASSEN

I see. He's supposed to make an appearance tonight, Utagawa, that is. At least that's what they tell me. You know, I saw your book in the bookstore the other day. There was a big display. I bought a copy, couldn't resist. I should tell you, as a piece of fiction, I rather enjoyed it. I bet you never imagined it would go on and have such a life of its own.

JOHN BELL

No. No, I didn't.

(*The sound of wooden clappers.*)

JOHN BELL

I didn't mean for things to go the way they did. That wasn't my intent.

OWEN MATTHIASSEN

You know, some of my colleagues, they become very skeptical when the author begins talking about intent, what he intended to do. They suspect the author's a bit of a liar in the first place. Why should they listen to him after the fact?

JOHN BELL

I don't remember writing what I wrote. It's like it was written by another person.

OWEN MATTHIASSEN

I've heard people say that. A speculative leap. But now, you see, one always hears that fiction is based on real life. Of course, that would mean you'd have to be a Japanese woman going on a thousand years old, give or take a few decades. As far as I can tell, you are not.

JOHN BELL

Maybe in a past life.

OWEN MATTHIASSEN

Come now. You can do better than that.

JOHN BELL

I just wrote what I wrote. I don't know where it came from. Maybe I was just inspired.

OWEN MATTHIASSEN

The muse descended from the ether, and whispered in your ear. And you, humble scribe, you just jotted it all down.

JOHN BELL

Something like that, yes.

OWEN MATTHIASSEN

It's fascinating, isn't it, how the human mind works, how it spins yarns, its infinite capacity for fabrication. Such literary talent, such business acumen. You surprise me, John, how far you've come. I never would have guessed you had it in you.

JOHN BELL

You don't really know me. You don't know me at all.

(*The sound of wooden clappers*)

OWEN MATTHIASSEN

No. No, I suppose I don't.

(*The sound of wooden clappers.*)

OWEN MATTHIASSEN

You know, there's something about his new work, I don't know what to make of it. There's something I don't quite understand. Perhaps it's generational. Or perhaps it's just me. Just a different way of seeing things. Either way, it's late, it's been a long day, and I should, I should get going. You must tell me if Utagawa shows up this time around. I'll be curious to hear.

(OWEN MATTHIASSEN *exits. The sound of wooden clappers.* JOHN BELL *disappears from view.*)

Scene 36

(*A stage.* DARIUS WHEELER *and* SETSUKO HEARN *appear. They stand apart. The sound of wooden clappers.*)

DARIUS WHEELER

So what happened to Darius Wheeler?

SETSUKO HEARN

He lived happily ever after. They all did, more or less.

DARIUS WHEELER

The guy lost his shirt.

SETSUKO HEARN

Not quite. There was one last twist. The manuscript he bought, the original that is, it wasn't what he thought it was.

DARIUS WHEELER

I thought it was a fake.

SETSUKO HEARN

It was. It was a fake Heian era manuscript. It was also an original work by a contemporary artist, a very popular, if somewhat reclusive painter.

(*The sound of wooden clappers.*)

DARIUS WHEELER

So did Utagawa, did he ever show up that night, in that last scene?

SETSUKO HEARN

Yes.

DARIUS WHEELER

What was he like?

SETSUKO HEARN

She. Utagawa turned out to be a she, a woman, a young woman. She'd been making her living restoring masterworks. She'd picked up quite a few techniques along the way. She'd actually, oddly enough, worked for Darius Wheeler at one point. They knew each other. In passing.

(*The sound of wooden clappers.*)

DARIUS WHEELER

And did he and that lady professor, did they ever—?

SETSUKO HEARN

No.

DARIUS WHEELER

That's too bad.

SETSUKO HEARN

He did just fine. She did just fine, too.

DARIUS WHEELER

Were they happy?

SETSUKO HEARN

Happy enough.

(*The sound of wooden clappers.*)

DARIUS WHEELER

So if, if I were to ask you to go for a drink later, you would say—

SETSUKO HEARN
Some other time.

DARIUS WHEELER
Right. Right.

(SETSUKO HEARN *approaches* DARIUS WHEELER, *touches the side of his face.*)

SETSUKO HEARN
Good night.

(*The sound of wooden clappers.* SETSUKO HEARN *turns and starts her exit. The sound of her footsteps across the stage.*)

DARIUS WHEELER
She turns. A memory pieces itself together in his mind. Her eyes. The look in her eyes. A picture forming as she recedes from view.

(*The 36 paintings shift their alignment to form a larger picture, like individual tiles of a larger mosaic. The picture they form is of a woman, a portrait of a lady, an echo of the lady from the top of the play, but different—part ancient, part contemporary, part Japanese woodblock print, part anime. Bright light on the portrait of the lady. The sound of wooden clappers. Darkness.*)

End of play.

The remainder of DARIUS WHEELER'S *Scene 1 monologue*

. . . And it's a miracle we even get there, driving through these insane mountain passes, and the whole time I'm thinking: I'm going to die, just wing it into oblivion on one of these switchbacks, one wrong move and that's it, that's all she wrote, my whole life is passing before my eyes, cause these Lahu guys, they're driving way too fast, wasted out of their minds on maekong whisky and Jack, and at the time, I, too, am wasted out of my mind, too wasted to see this place for what it is—

Because the thing is, all right, it's beautiful country, indescribably beautiful, and maybe ten white guys have ever seen it before, like no place else in the world, rows and rows of emerald green paddy fields, Pai river coming down from way up north, the water this dark green, deep, the color of tea—

It's nightfall when we get to where we're going, tiny Shan village, tattooed Shan guys standing around with AK-47s, smell of fire and jhoss sticks burning, I pay my guides a few thousand baht for their trouble, light up a smoke, wait for my contact, friend of a friend, hooked up with him in Bangkok, crazy Australian guy—"I hear you have an interest in Asian antiquities," is how it all began. I didn't know this guy from Adam, dumb, in retrospect, very, very dumb, and it's getting darker and darker, and it's dawning on me my situation, when finally I see him in the distance, driving up with his men, and I see in the flatbed of his truck he's got all these crates and his men start unloading the crates, prying them open, and I get a look at what he has . . .